WHAT THE CUTS CUT

A FIELD GUIDE TO THE HIDDEN HARM OF GOVERNMENT DOWNSIZING

NICCO MELE

MARJORIE STERNE

JPZ
J. P. Zenger Books

Formatted with Vellum

CONTENTS

INTRODUCTION

HOW TO USE THIS BOOK

A Field Guide to What the Cuts Really Mean

Most of us don't think about public policy every day. But we all wonder things like: *Is this lettuce safe to eat? What if my kid gets bullied at school? When is that bridge going to be repaired? What if my electric bill just keeps going up? Who can we call after a natural disaster? Why is everything getting more expensive? Is my pension safe?*

Those questions aren't hypothetical. And the answers to them are the real-world results of decisions being made in Washington every day. So, we built this book around those questions, and hundreds of questions like them, that swirl through people's minds all the time about the things everyone cares about:

- Your home
- Your family
- Your health
- Your job
- Your commute
- Your community

You can open this book to the chapter that matches what's on your mind right now – schools, food, public safety, healthcare – and find clear answers to a direct question:

What do these cuts really mean in everyday life?

This book, like the questions it's built around, doesn't care about your party affiliation or require any specialized education. You don't need to know how the federal budget works, or the names of dozens of government agencies, to understand what happens when:

- the warning comes too late;
- the bridge isn't fixed;
- the loan disappears;
- the hospital shuts its doors;
- the help never arrives.

WHAT YOU'LL FIND IN EACH CHAPTER

Every chapter follows the same basic structure:

Everyday problems first: We start with lived experience, not politics. No acronyms, no legislative jargon—just what people feel when something breaks, disappears, or gets harder to afford.

What changed—and how: Then we explain what actually happened behind the scenes. Not just budgets, but staffing losses, enforcement pullbacks, privatization, and new barriers that quietly shut people out.

Why it matters beyond one person: Cuts don't stop with one family. They ripple outward—into local economies, public safety, housing values, prices, and long-term opportunity.

A clear bottom line: Each chapter ends with a short takeaway you can remember, repeat, and use anytime that you want to talk about these things.

ONE LAST THING

You may not recognize every agency name in this book. That's okay.

What matters isn't memorizing who does what. What matters is seeing the connection: when public systems are weakened, everyday life gets riskier, more expensive, and less predictable—often without warning.

This book is here to make those connections visible.

Use it when you need answers.

Use it when you need language.

Use it when someone says, *"I don't see how this affects me."*

Chances are, it already does.

CHAPTER 1
YOUR HOME SWEET HOME

FEMA, NOAA, ZONING, PARKS, FAA NOISE REGULATIONS, HUD PROGRAMS

For most Americans, "home" isn't only where they live —raise their kids, celebrate the good times, and have the hard conversations - it's also their biggest investment. It's where wealth is built, passed on, and protected. But what many homeowners don't realize is that the value and safety of their home depend on government programs they probably never think about.

Getting the financing to buy a home?

- More than 25% of new mortgages are backed by government programs run by the Federal Housing Authority (FHA), the Department of Agriculture (USDA), and the Department of Veterans Affairs.

Protecting your home and property from extreme weather?

- The National Oceanic and Atmospheric Association gives homeowners detailed and accurate advanced forecasts, and when disaster does happen, FEMA is (was) there to reopen roads, help get utilities running again, and even help owners bear the costs of repairs and rebuilding.

And don't forget the liveability of your property, your neighborhood, and your town.

- Lots of federal funding and government rules improve your quality of life in your own home. For example, Federal Aviation Administration rules minimize noise pollution from nearby airports, and the Department of the Interior distributes funds and grants for parks and green spaces. The Environmental Protection Agency protects the stream that runs behind your house from becoming polluted.

If these programs get cut, fewer Americans will be able to purchase a home, and the homes they already own could become harder to insure, harder to sell, more vulnerable to disasters, or even lose value—fast.

What if I can't get a mortgage?

What if you have a good job and some savings, but you're a young family and don't have much credit history? What if you're a farmer and you want to start your own farm in your hometown, where rental homes don't even exist and wages are low? What if you're a military veteran who served the country overseas for years, but doesn't have much or anything else to show a lender in terms of employment history?... How will you get a mortgage?

Whether you're a small business owner, a college professor, an ex-marine, or a ballet dancer, you probably want a home of your own. A place to raise a family, or a garden, to display your poster collection, listen to your music, prepare your meals... A place where you can paint the walls any color you want and even tear one down if it's standing between you and the way you want your space to be. Homeownership is a huge part of the American Dream and a cornerstone of American communities.

When the Federal Housing Authority was established in the aftermath of the Great Depression, only one in ten American families owned their home, and would-be homebuyers had to come up with a 50% or more down payment in order to get a mortgage for the rest. The Veterans Affairs loan program was created, as part of the GI Bill, in 1944 to help returning soldiers reestablish themselves and start and raise their families in US communities. These mortgage programs helped expand the number of the American middle class, and provided the stability that contributed to the population growth - the baby-boom - of the late 1940s and 1950s.

More than 25% of new mortgages in America are backed by government programs like FHA, VA, or USDA. If you're a first-time homebuyer, a veteran, or someone buying in a rural area, these loan programs might be the only reason you were able to afford a home in the first place. And, if you are a homeowner with equity in your home, their support of the housing market is a big part of the reason your home retains its value.

Now, all of these mortgage programs are at risk due to real and proposed federal budget cuts, even though they remain foundational to both buyers' ability to obtain mortgages and the health of the housing market overall. Despite operating at a profit - The FHA is funded through mortgage insurance premiums - the FHA has been targeted for both budget and staff cuts, which would impact its abilities both to liaise between would-be buyers and lenders and to service existing FHA-backed mortgages. Support for service members and spouses who obtained mortgages through the VA home loan program has whipsawed between seeing a foreclosure prevention program abruptly terminated in early 2025 and new legislation which might restore some support, but has had spotty implementation. And, the administration has proposed eliminating the USDA Direct Home Loans altogether, while severely reducing funding for rural home repair grants, rural housing vouchers, and other loan programs that benefit rural and low-income homebuyers.

What could these cuts mean for me (or my kids)?

Mortgages are already hard to get. Right now, record-high numbers of young adults are living at home well into their 30's, delaying home ownership and forming families. And mortgages could become harder to get - and come with more complex terms - as cuts to the FHA, the USDA, and the VA housing programs go through. Lenders could raise interest rates. Down payments could skyrocket. Default assistance and forbearance options could disappear. And fewer people being able to buy homes doesn't just mean they can't get one. It also means it'll be harder to find a buyer when you want to sell the home you have.

Who's backing my mortgage?

The FHA insures mortgages issued by private lenders. By insuring the mortgage, the FHA enables borrowers with less credit history, lower credit scores, or less to spend on a down payment to secure financing, at reasonable interest rates, through private lenders who might otherwise consider them too high risk.

The FHA is a profitable branch of HUD and operates primarily on the income it earns through mortgage insurance premiums - it is not a burden on taxpayers. The USDA has (had) two programs to assist low and very low-income rural homebuyers, and to encourage community development in rural areas - USDA Guaranteed Home Loans and USDA Direct Home Loans. These programs guaranteed loans for low and very low-income homebuyers without access to safe and sanitary housing, offering zero downpayment mortgages, covering closing costs, and, in the case of direct home loans, offering mortgage repayment assistance.

FHA was created to revive the housing industry and advance home ownership in the wake of the Great Depression. At that time, most home mortgage lenders required a 50% downpayment on a mortgage, and only 1 in 10 American families owned their home. During the foreclosure crisis/great recession/financial crisis of 2008, the FHA played a key role in preventing more widespread damage to the housing market, and keeping mortgage funding available even as many financial institutions were damaged.

The Department of Veterans Affairs loan program has assisted more than 24 million veterans in achieving home ownership since its inception in 1944. The VA offers direct loans and loan guarantees for veterans.

Advantages of VA loans include no down payment requirement loans, no mortgage insurance requirements, low and fixed interest rates, lower or no minimum credit score, and VA cash-out refinancing. (VA loans are also transferable in the event of a sale of the home, even if the buyer is not a veteran; the better terms of a VA mortgage would likely appeal to other buyers as well.) VA and FHA mortgage guarantees are credited with increasing the number of baby boomers.

What if my neighborhood just… changed?

What if they build a data center in town? What if our local airport reroutes flights over your house? What if the road drainage isn't maintained? What if the playground down the block is closed? What if the local park goes to seed or is sold off?

Your home's value isn't just about square footage or granite countertops. It's about what's nearby: clean air, a quiet street, a park down the block, good zoning rules.

Of course, you know that a nice quiet area with access to green space and waterways adds to your quality of life and your enjoyment of your home and your town. But did you know that these amenities are maintained and supported by a variety of federal programs that provide the funding for, for example, the creation and maintenance of parks? They also establish the rules that limit noise pollution, from airplanes overhead, for example, and guard against pollution that can be destructive to both your property and your health.

But all of that is facing cuts. Vehicle emissions and clean air rules are being actively rolled back. Permits for the construction of polluting industrial sites are being expedited. And, funding for the creation and maintenance of parks and green spaces is diverted.

What could this mean for you? Your local park might close, be sold to developers, or cease to be maintained at the same levels of cleanliness and safety. The creek behind your house could get polluted. Jet noise could get worse. Zoning and fair housing laws might be weakened—meaning new industrial buildings, short-term rentals, and discriminatory HOAs could spring up around your city. Those things aren't just annoying. They can make you think twice about whether you want to live in that town. They can also tank your property value.

What if no one warned me a storm was coming?

If the National Weather Service were privatized, how would we know the forecast? What if good forecasting were only available to people who could pay for it? What if every forecast was so different you couldn't tell which to believe?

What if you needed to close your shutters, clear your yard, lay in supplies, or even evacuate ahead of a snow storm, hurricane, wildfire, or flood? You'd want as much warning as possible, *right?*

We all want to live on the water, by the lake, in the woods, on the bluff, at the ranch, by the river...

Most of our homes, and most of the most expensive real estate in the country, are located in areas at risk of severe weather events. Almost 40% of us live in coastal areas, more than 100 million of us live in areas at risk of wildfire, more than 40% of us live in areas with flood risks. And, in a recent survey conducted by the PEW research center, 72% of respondents reported having experienced at least one extreme weather event in 2023-2024.

Right now, the National Oceanic and Atmospheric Administration (NOAA) helps us prepare for, and protect ourselves from, severe weather. It predicts severe weather, tracks storms, and notifies you and your state and local government before they hit. That means you can protect yourself, your family, and your property. It also enables your federal, state, and local governments to prepare in advance and position manpower, tools, and resources where they will be most needed. Sometimes, this means your state governor knows when to dedicate state resources to opening life-saving cooling and warming centers during periods of extreme heat and cold. At other times, it means that electric and road crews are put in position in advance to reopen your street and get your lights back on after a big storm.

Thirty years ago, the "Storm of the Century"—also known as the 1993 Superstorm or Blizzard of '93—struck the eastern United States, becoming one of the most powerful winter storms in U.S. history. From March 12–14, the storm unleashed record-breaking snowfall, subzero temperatures, and hurricane-force winds across a third of the nation, while also spawning tornadoes in Florida and driving a deadly storm surge into its Gulf Coast. More than 250 lives were lost, over $3 billion in damages were incurred, and commercial air travel ground to a halt. Despite the scale of destruction, the toll would have been far worse without the National Weather Service's newly modernized forecasting tools, which marked a turning point in the use of numerical weather prediction. Though satellite technology was still evolving, NOAA satellites delivered critical data that helped forecasters monitor the storm from its explosive formation to its final retreat.

Thanks to NOAA's accurate observations and widespread forecasting, officials up and down the coast were able to prepare - declare states of emergency to free resources, close highways before motorists could become trapped in the snow, deploy public safety workers, and more.

NOAA has continued to provide advanced and accurate forecasting that saves homes and lives. In 2024, NOAA's forecasts helped 5 million people get out of Hurricane Helene's path. In 2005, it helped 1.5 million flee Katrina. Those are lives and homes saved.

What does this mean in everyday life? Can you imagine going back to only short-term forecasts? Or having to pay private companies for life-saving weather forecasting? The technology for which has been federally funded and developed since the dawn of our nation?

Proposed budget cuts would have cost the NOAA $1.5 billion, almost 50% of its budget. Weather centers, including the National Storm Center, would be closed. And as Congress continues to debate that budget, more than 1,000 NOAA employees are already gone. Some plans even suggested turning storm forecasting entirely over to private companies or individual states, which don't have the equipment or experience to do the job.

You, and millions like you, might not get a reliable warning in time to prepare for a storm. And, if your home, like hundreds of millions of others, is in a floodplain or hurricane zone, that uncertainty could make it harder to insure your home, and even drive down your property value.

What if a storm seriously damages my town -- Will anyone come to help?

What if your southern town is trapped by snow and ice? What if half of the trees in your mountain community fall across the road? What if the river floods and washes away your roads, bridges, and possibly even your home? What if the wind carries wildfire into your city? What if you can't afford to rebuild after a storm?

We're pretty good at anticipating the weather, but we can't stop it from coming. Most of us have experienced some kind of extreme weather and some of its costs: The thousands of miles of roads washed away in Appalachia because of Hurricane Helene, the thousands of homes lost to the LA wildfires, trees uprooted, and whole buildings torn from their foundations by tornadoes in Arkansas. By FEMA's own data, the majority of us live in areas at risk of severe weather events of some kind. It's not always the kind of weather your state can be expected to prepare for. (The 2026 snow and ice storms across the southeast- should those states have had standing supplies of salt, plows, and shovels?) And, it can be the case that damage to homes and infrastructure is so severe that there is no way the state alone - the state just hit by disaster - can reach affected communities and repair damage.

So what does FEMA do?

In the immediate aftermath of a storm, FEMA:

- Runs search and rescue missions
- Reopens roads
- Helps to get utilities working again
- Provides for basic human needs like shelter, clean water, and food
- Can provide free or low-cost housing for storm victims whose homes are damaged or unreachable

When it's time to repair and rebuild, FEMA:

- Can offer financing to homeowners to repair and rebuild
- Can finance the repair and rebuilding of public structures like post offices, schools, and government buildings

Our federal government has provided some form of disaster relief for hundreds of years. It includes both financial support for states, individuals, and businesses, *and* physical support that includes supplies, machinery, expertise, and real boots on the ground reopening roads, testing the water supply, and distributing blankets and food. This support saves lives and prevents entire communities from being wiped off the map in the aftermath of natural disasters.

Until recently, we were also on a path that prioritized building infrastructure that could withstand severe weather better. The Building Resilient Infrastructure and Communities (BRIC) funding allocated through the Infrastructure Improvement and Jobs Act was allocated to make sure that our roads, bridges, and public buildings are made with modern materials that can stand up to more heat, rain, snow, wind, ice, or whatever else Mother Nature wants to throw at them. But even that, an investment in disaster preparedness that would save money in the future, is facing cuts.

Despite the fact that federal involvement in disaster recovery isn't charity - our economy and national security depend on maintaining the productivity and interconnectedness of our territory - that safety net is disappearing. FEMA has already lost hundreds of staff, and more than $600 million in disaster relief programs are on the chopping block. Plans are in motion to end the National Flood Insurance Program. This would, if successful, leave homeowners no option outside of the private insurance marketplace—meaning companies could refuse coverage in high-risk areas or raise prices sky-high. And States across the country are already seeing drastic cuts to federal disaster relief, having their declared states of emergencies denied or seeing disaster relief funds tied to unrelated requests from the federal government.

What if I can't afford to rebuild?

Let's say the worst happens. A tornado hits your neighborhood. A flood ruins your basement. A wildfire scorches your roof.

You'd probably call your insurance company first. But what if the payout doesn't cover the damage? Or what if your deductible is so high you can't afford to start repairs?

That's one of the places where FEMA usually steps in. After disasters like Hurricane Katrina, FEMA helped hundreds of thousands of people repair or rebuild their homes. Sometimes, FEMA funding can help cover the "named storm deductible" when their estimate of the damages exceeds the estimate provided by your insurance provider.

What cuts to this support could mean for you -

If your home is hit by a disaster, you may be left to cover repairs entirely on your own—or be denied flood insurance altogether. That could force you into debt or even foreclosure.

Bottom Line

The truth is, your home's value, safety, and livability are propped up by public systems—systems most of us rarely think about. Cuts to these programs don't just "reduce spending." They raise your risk. They reduce your security. And they could end up costing you far more than any government program ever did.

If the storm comes, and no one warns you… if you can't get a loan… if you can't afford to rebuild… if your neighborhood starts to slide…

You'll find out just how much your home was worth—and how much it depended on the things we're now cutting.

CHAPTER 2

YOUR HEALTHCARE: DOCTOR'S ORDERS

NIH RESEARCH, HOSPITAL FUNDING, MEDICARE, MEDICAID

Government funding is the hidden foundation of our nation's health. Our tax dollars pay to prevent diseases, find cures for illnesses, and make sure people get medical care. Even if you have private insurance, these services are very important for your health and safety. They pay for amazing research that leads to new medicines and treatments. They also watch out for and control public health dangers, and they create a vital safety net that helps the elderly and less well-off access healthcare and supports hospitals and clinics. Combined, these investments keep us safer, develop cutting-edge treatments, and ensure access to healthcare.

How does it work?

Preventing disease:

- The Centers for Disease Control and Prevention (CDC) tracks and prevents the spread of disease, releases vaccine schedules, monitors public health risks, and releases public warnings and guidance.

Finding cures:

- The National Institute of Health (NIH) is the largest funder of biomedical research in the world. Medical research in the 20th century has added more than 30 years to life expectancy in the developed countries.

Providing treatment:

- Medicaid and Medicare provide healthcare services to the poor, retirees, and the elderly. More than 40% of births are funded with Medicaid, as is more than 50% of long-term care.

How do I keep my family safe and healthy?

Do my kids really need all these shots? I'm 37 and healthy, do I need to get vaccinated this winter? What if there's a new flu or other virus around? How will I know? I'm feeling unwell and have strange symptoms. Who can help me find out what's wrong?

The Centers for Disease Control and Prevention promotes public health by controlling and preventing the spread of disease. It accomplishes this through research into both the evolution and spread of diseases as well as treatments, running public information campaigns that warn us of the spread of potentially contagious diseases and harmful pollutants, and acts as a first responder during public health emergencies. It is thanks to the CDC that children across the country are regularly vaccinated against infectious, and often deadly diseases, like measles. Thanks to the CDC, we know how to prevent the spread of STDs. CDC grants fund addiction treatment centers, disease tracking, and drinking water testing. In short, the CDC saves lives by preventing people from getting sick in the first place.

Budget and staff cuts at the CDC not only hamper pandemic preparedness, they will immediately affect children's access to vaccinations, lead poisoning testing, and public awareness of health risks.

What shots does my baby need, and when?

The CDC creates the vaccination schedule that helps protect kids from serious diseases like measles. It helps states run vaccination programs for both children and adults. And, its recommendations ensure that the cost of vaccines remains covered by insurance.

But, right now, American families are getting mixed messages from the CDC about vaccines and vaccine schedules. Seven vaccines were removed from the list of recommended vaccines - despite the fact that they protect against contagious and potentially fatal illnesses - and were relegated to the grey area called "shared clinical decision" making. The mixed messages, delayed communications, and what sometimes sound like directly contradictory advice from officials in the Department of Health and Human Services have, understandably, left a lot of families confused and hesitant about making decisions for their children's vaccination schedules.

Meanwhile, we're seeing a rise in ~~the~~ hospitalizations and deaths of children from diseases that are preventable. In 2025, the US had the highest number of cases of measles that we've seen in three decades, and the disease is continuing to spread in 2026. With the CDC's budget and staff cuts, and priority changes, even fewer kids may get their vaccines on time. This could lead to a return of diseases we've already worked hard to prevent, putting children at risk and weakening community protection.

What if a new flu strain starts spreading — who will warn us?

The CDC is also the main agency tracking how diseases spread and evolve, including new flu strains. It researches viruses and runs public warning systems so you know when there's a health risk. Budget and staff cuts at the CDC will slow down or stop that work, leaving communities with less warning and fewer tools - including updated flu vaccines - to fight outbreaks. That means you and your family could be left unprotected.

How do I know it's safe to drink the water?

The CDC plays a key role in making sure your drinking water is safe and in notifying the public of potentially dangerous contaminants in drinking water. It does this by funding and conducting water quality tests and giving grants to communities to support clean water programs. But the giant cuts proposed to the CDC's budget would take away the resources needed to keep doing this work. That means less testing, fewer protections, and a greater risk of harmful pollutants in your water.

What if I think I've been exposed to something dangerous — who helps me find out?

If you think you've been exposed to something

harmful, like lead, the CDC is one of the first places to turn. It provides expert guidance, supports testing, and responds to health scares. Budget cuts make it harder for the CDC to respond quickly or offer the help you need—leaving more people without answers during a crisis.

Will there ever be a cure or new treatment for... cancer, Alzheimers, Parkinsons, bipolar disorder?

What if I am diagnosed with a serious illness? Will there be a cure in time? My Doctor says I need to be tested for an illness, but the test is expensive and painful - will it ever get better? Will I have to stay in the hospital after I get a knee or hip replacement? What are new hips and knees made of anyway?

Whatever your thoughts about the healthcare system in our country, it is undeniable that we are a global leader in health sciences research and a leading exporter of medical technologies. This is largely thanks to the National Institute of Health (NIH), our premier medical research institute, a vital source of financial support for medical research at US Universities, and the largest funder of biomedical research in the world. NIH-funded research has provided the foundation for innumerable breakthrough therapies in everything from infertility to cancer to Alzheimer's disease.

But there is a long road between research and the development of a safe and effective treatment that can be manufactured and delivered at scale. It can be between 17 and 20 years. Twenty years ago, scientists doing basic research began to look into the blood of Alzheimer's patients. Just recently, the FDA approved the first-ever blood test for Alzheimer's. This breakthrough will save patients thousands of dollars previously spent on PET scans and painful spinal taps. And, more importantly, it means people will be diagnosed sooner and begin treatment earlier.

What if I get cancer --- will there be a cure in time?

Cures for every disease start in a research lab. The National Institutes of Health (NIH) is the biggest funder of medical research in the world, and its work is essential to finding cures for diseases like cancer. Most of its $47.7 billion 2024 budget went to support research at hospitals, universities, and labs across the U.S. That research helps us understand how diseases work and develop new treatments. But major cuts proposed for NIH—including a 40% reduction in the budget and the cancellation of 694 research grants worth $2.7 billion—are already shutting down labs and stopping important research. These cuts could slow down or even stop the discovery of new treatments, making it harder to get life-saving care when you or someone you love needs it most.

What if my kid gets diagnosed with autism --- what treatments will help?

NIH-funded research has played a big role in helping us understand autism and develop treatments for it. But creating a safe and effective treatment takes a long time—often 17 to 20 years. With the massive cuts in NIH, there will be less money for the early research that makes these breakthroughs possible. That means new and better autism treatments could take longer to develop, leaving fewer options to help your child. The NIH also runs programs like REACH and the Small Business Program, which help turn promising discoveries into real treatments by moving them into testing and development. Without this support, many good ideas might never reach the people who need them.

What if I want to have children, but can't?

NIH-funded research has produced many important medical breakthroughs, including treatments that help people facing infertility. The progress we've made in helping people have children comes from years of careful research into reproductive health. But with cuts to NIH funding, research into infertility could slow down or stop. That means fewer new options for people trying to start a family, making the journey to parenthood harder and more stressful—both emotionally and financially.

What if I develop Alzheimer's like my mom did --- will there be a test, or even a treatment?

Important progress in Alzheimer's research—like the first-ever blood test to help diagnose the disease—has come from years of NIH-funded work. This new test is less invasive and much cheaper than older methods, saving patients thousands of dollars. But with NIH budget cuts, research like this is at risk. These cuts could slow down or stop work on better tests and treatments for Alzheimer's, making it harder to find new breakthroughs that could bring hope and improve life for people living with the disease.

What if a new virus shows up --- who's studying it right now?

The NIH plays an absolutely critical role in studying emerging infectious diseases and developing rapid responses to potential pandemics. Their research provides the essential foundation for understanding new viruses, developing effective vaccines, and creating life-saving treatments. If NIH funding is cut, the nation's capacity to quickly and effectively respond to new viral threats would be severely diminished. This could leave the country vulnerable to widespread outbreaks, leading to significant impacts on public health and safety on a massive scale. Our ability to identify, track, and combat new pathogens relies heavily on consistent and robust investment in biomedical research.

Real and proposed cuts to NIH and NIH funding for medical research put not only our primacy as a hub of medical research and the enviable achievements of our research universities at risk, they put our lives at risk.

Where is healthcare when we need it most?

How will we pay for our parents' care when we can't take care of them anymore? What if my newborn needs special care? What happens if I lose my job, or after I retire - How will I afford my healthcare? Can our local hospital or clinic afford to stay open if Medicaid is cut?

Medicaid and Medicare provide essential access to healthcare for huge swaths of the population, and in doing so, they also financially support hospitals, clinics, and nursing homes across the country. 40% of all births in the US are covered by Medicaid. 49% of all children are covered by "CHIP", the Child Health Insurance Program. Tens of millions of senior citizens are on Medicare, and the number of enrollees is growing exponentially as the baby-boom generation ages. More than 60% of all seniors living in long-term care rely on Medicaid to pay for their care. *And,* more than 30 million working-age Americans rely on Medicaid and Medicaid expansion for access to healthcare.

It may not be enough, but we do have some forms of government-sponsored healthcare available to people in every stage of life. These include:

CHIP:

- The Child Health Insurance Program under mMedicaid provides coverage for 49% of all children in the US.

Medicaid and Medicaid Expansion:

- Provides access to healthcare for more than 70 million low-income Americans.

Medicare:

- Guarantees healthcare to people over the age of 65, providing coverage in the years between retirement and entrance into long-term care.

Medicaid for Seniors:

- Medicaid covers long-term care costs for more than half of all nursing home residents.

These government programs provide a lifeline for Americans at their most vulnerable, whether it's an infant in a cradle, or her grandfather with a rollator. They also support healthcare and related jobs across the country, and, in many places, are the only reason medical facilities can afford to operate at all.

When you hear or read about cuts to government-sponsored healthcare, you are probably wondering...

What happens when my mom needs a nursing home — how will we pay for it?

Medicaid helps pay for long-term care in nursing homes—something Medicare doesn't cover for extended stays. Over half of nursing home residents rely on Medicaid. With the Medicaid cuts in the Big Beautiful Bill Act, many families could be left struggling to pay or unable to find care for their elderly loved ones. It is estimated that at least 600 nursing homes will close. More than half of all nursing home residents are on Medicaid, and 12% are on Medicare.

(Medicare exclusively covers short stays and medical treatments, whereas Medicaid covers long-term care and social wellness programs.

What if I lose my job and still need to see a doctor?

If you lose your job, Medicaid and CHIP can help cover healthcare for you and your children. More than 70 million Americans depend on these programs. The Medicaid cuts in the Big Beautiful Bill Act mean fewer people will qualify and or fewer services will be covered—leaving many without medical care when they need it most.

What if my baby is born premature — who helps pay for their care?

Medicaid pays for more than 40% of births in the U.S. —and even more in rural and southern states. Premature babies often need expensive, life-saving care. With Medicaid funding being reduced, that help could disappear, putting financial pressure on parents and risking the health of newborns.

What if I have private insurance but the local hospital closes?

Even with private insurance, you could lose access to care if your local hospital shuts down. Hospitals rely on Medicaid and Medicare for more than half of their revenues or income. Big cuts to these programs will force hospitals to reduce services or close—especially in rural or lower-income areas—leaving you without emergency care close to home.

What happens when I turn 65 — will I still be able to see a doctor?

Medicare provides health insurance for people 65 and older. Right now, about 68.5 million Americans rely on it, and that number is growing fast. 11,400 members of the baby boom generation are turning 65 - and becoming eligible for Medicare - every day. By 2030, as many as 80 million Americans could rely on Medicare for healthcare. That's almost a quarter of the US population. Budget cuts mean fewer doctors will accept Medicare patients – and longer wait times for those who do. That would make it harder and more expensive for seniors to get the care they need.

Does this really matter in my town, city, or state?

Sure, the most important part of government-sponsored healthcare is that it provides access to care for people who can't otherwise get it. But, it is also very, very important to state and local economies. Think about your local hospital and what goes on in and around it - There are doctors and nurses and administrators. There is laundry service. There is food service. There are gift shops and florists either inside or nearby. There are groundskeepers and janitorial staff. There is a constant movement of trucks and vans bringing in necessary supplies. There are specialists in waste disposal carefully taking potentially dangerous materials away. *All* of these, and many more, are state and local jobs that depend on the hospital itself.

What happens when the hospital, or local doctors' offices, or clinics, that depend on Medicaid for large percentages of their income, no longer have that income? They cut back. And when they do, it doesn't just affect the people who lose their jobs, it affects the other businesses in town where those people used to shop. It affects the town's ability to raise money through income and sales tax. It leaves less money for the city to spend on maintaining roads and schools. A 2025 study from the Commonwealth Fund found that cuts in Medicaid and SNAP could shrink state economies by a combined $113 billion in the first year alone.

What Happens When Medicaid and Food Assistance Are Cut

A new study from the Commonwealth Fund looks at what would happen if the federal government makes deep cuts to Medicaid (health coverage for low-income people, seniors, and people with disabilities) and SNAP (food assistance, often called food stamps). The short version: cutting these programs doesn't just hurt families who rely on them — it hurts entire local economies.

The researchers studied a budget plan that would cut nearly $900 billion from Medicaid and over $200 billion from SNAP over the next decade. They used economic models to see how those cuts would ripple through states and communities.

Here's what they found.

Job Losses — Far Beyond Healthcare and Food

In just one year (2026), the cuts would likely cause more than 1 million jobs to disappear nationwide. These aren't just government jobs. Nearly 500,000 healthcare workers could lose their jobs — nurses, aides, hospital staff, and people who work in clinics and nursing homes. About 80,000 food-related jobs could disappear — including grocery stores, food suppliers, and local farmers. Hundreds of thousands of additional jobs would be lost in retail, transportation, and other local businesses that depend on people spending money in their communities. When people lose health coverage or food assistance, they spend less — and when spending drops, businesses cut back or shut down.

Smaller Local Economies, Less Money for Schools and Roads

The study found that these cuts would shrink state economies by about $113 billion in a single year — more than the federal government would actually save. States and cities would also collect almost $9 billion less in tax revenue, because fewer people would be working and spending money.

That means:

- Less money for schools
- Less money for roads and public transit
- Less money for emergency services
- More pressure on state and local budgets, especially in rural areas and small towns

Almost every state would be hit — red states and blue states alike.

Cuts Cost More Than They Save

One of the most important findings is this: Cutting Medicaid and SNAP doesn't just reduce government spending — it creates new economic damage.

When federal dollars disappear:

- Hospitals and nursing homes close or lay off staff
- Grocery stores and local businesses lose customers
- States collect less tax revenue
- Communities are forced to cut services or raise taxes

The study also warns that if additional health coverage supports expire, job losses could grow even larger — pushing total losses closer to 1.3 million jobs.

Bottom Line

Federal funding is important to the entire healthcare system in our country. Thanks to NIH funding, our research institutes are the pillars of advancement in medical science. We find cures and develop treatments. Thanks to the CDC, we prevent outbreaks before they happen. We are immunized against contagious illnesses, and we are kept informed about pending threats. And, thanks to Medicaid and Medicare, we are able to provide care to the most vulnerable among us. When funding for these programs is cut, it is not just an attack on researchers, doctors, and bureaucrats. It is an attack on the health and safety - the very lives - of all of us.

Medicaid and SNAP aren't just "safety net" programs for people in crisis. They are economic engines that keep hospitals open, workers employed, and local economies moving. When these programs are cut, the harm doesn't stay contained. It spreads — to workers, businesses, schools, and entire communities. Cuts don't just take help away from people who need it. They take jobs, money, and stability away from all of us.

CHAPTER 3
YOUR TRANSPORTATION: ROADS, RAILS, AND RESCUE TEAMS

DOT, HIGHWAYS, FAA, AMTRAK, EMERGENCY SERVICES

The US has the largest road network of any country in the world. Our highways, freeways, and local roads combined cover more than 4 million miles. We don't think about it often, but the highway system is essential to our daily routines—getting us to work, school, and appointments. It is important to our national and local economies. It facilitates trade between states, supports jobs in freight, trucking, and construction, brings tourism to rural areas, and facilitates suburban and rural living as a lifestyle option for Americans. Our roads, highways, and airways are also extraordinarily important to our national security - facilitating our ability to quickly move resources in the event of an emergency.

But, policy changes at the current Department of Transportation (DOT) roll back decades of progress on building stronger roads and bridges, managing pollution, streamlining commutes, and simply making our communities more livable. The DOT is rolling back clean air and water protections, flood prevention efforts, and the walkability and bikeability of urban and suburban neighborhoods. They have blocked and unblocked funding for major urban connectivity projects in New York, Texas, and California, leaving both commuters and city planners in constant uncertainty.

Meanwhile, rural and tribal communities—already underserved—face new barriers to interconnected transit as infrastructure funding that once focused on providing less-advantaged communities with the connectivity they need disappears. At the same time, urban parks, often essential in economically disadvantaged areas, may go unfunded, and clean-up projects for polluted or hazardous areas may be abandoned.

Instead of giving money based on where it's most needed, the federal government has been weaponizing transportation funding to try to convince people and states to comply with its political agenda. For example, the administration has attempted to impose new rules that say states can only get transportation funding if they meet certain requirements—like charging tolls, having high birth rates, or helping enforce federal immigration laws. States that try to limit carbon pollution or have public health rules more stringent than those of the administration, like vaccine or mask requirements, could lose transportation funding. These changes hurt not only our ability to safely and easily get to our jobs and school, they also hurt our air, our water, and the places we call home.

Your Roads & Bridges

What if the road I drive on every day is starting to crumble? When was the last time someone checked to see how this bridge was holding up? Why does it seem like the roads are flooded every time it just rains a few drops? What is this new pavement made of? Are they ever going to finish the sidewalks in my neighborhood? How will our town pay to maintain the roads going in and out of town?

It's no joke how much we rely on our nationwide network of interconnected highways and roadways. Even if, on normal days, the road itself is the last thing you're thinking about as you drive on it on your way to wherever you're going, it being damaged or just backed up with traffic can ruin your day pretty quickly.

In the fall of 2024, Hurricane Helene brought massive destruction to roads and bridges throughout Appalachia, a region that includes 13 states and stretches from Pennsylvania to Alabama. 6,000 miles of roads were destroyed in North Carolina alone. Bridges were washed away. Entire towns were completely isolated from each other and the rest of the country.

That kind of damage doesn't just mean people couldn't get to school or work. It means no mail service, no packages, no deliveries to local stores. It means no family members are coming to visit. In the Carolinas and other states on the southern end of the Appalachian Trail, it has also meant a lot of lost revenue from tourism that hasn't yet fully rebounded, even months after the disaster.

What if the road to my job is no longer maintained, or if the bridge I drive over every day starts to crumble?

Your safety could be at risk. The Federal Highway Administration (FHWA) funds 25% of all road construction and maintenance in the country. While the overall transportation budget might see an increase, policy changes are shifting funds away from maintenance and research into safer roads and materials. This means the road you rely on for your daily commute might not receive the necessary upkeep, leading to deterioration and potentially unsafe driving conditions. The shift in funding priorities away from infrastructure maintenance and research into sustainable and resilient materials means that bridges, like roads, may not receive the necessary attention. A crumbling bridge is a direct safety hazard, and without adequate funding for inspection and repair, the risk of such hazards increases.

What if my community doesn't have sidewalks or crosswalks?

Your community may have a harder time getting them. The new policies favor projects with a large-scale economic impact, which often means that smaller-scale projects like sidewalks and crosswalks, especially in smaller towns or less populated areas, may not get funded. Additionally, the move away from so-called "equity" initiatives could disproportionately affect low-income communities that have historically been under-resourced in terms of pedestrian infrastructure.

What if the roads are flooded or blocked—who clears them?

While the responsibility for clearing roads typically falls to state and local transportation departments, federal funding plays a significant role in their ability to respond effectively. The policy changes that de-emphasize resilient infrastructure could leave communities more vulnerable to the impacts of extreme weather events. If roads are not built or maintained to withstand flooding, they are more likely to become impassable, and the resources available to clear them may be strained.

What if my city can't get funds for safer roads because it's considered too "diverse" or too small?

This is a real possibility under the new policies. The anti-equity stance means that projects in areas deemed too small to have a "macroeconomic impact" may not receive support. These communities are often rural or urban neighborhoods with high proportions of people of color, immigrants, and low-income residents. Individuals in these communities often face compounded challenges and may lack political influence, making it difficult for them to secure necessary resources and support for safer roads.

What if nobody's researching safer roads, better traffic flow, or stronger materials anymore?

This would have long-term negative consequences for our entire transportation system. The FHWA has historically funded research into these critical areas. A lack of ongoing research means we will be slower to adopt solutions that can save lives, reduce congestion, and build a more resilient infrastructure. This stagnation would not only impact safety but also our global economic competitiveness.

"WHEN HEAT STOPS TRAFFIC: THE 2024 THIRD AVENUE BRIDGE INCIDENT"

On July 8 of 2024, the 3rd Avenue Bridge in Manhattan - a major commercial and commuting artery between the Bronx and Manhattan and also a "swing bridge" which swings open to allow the passage of commercial vessels - became so swollen from the summer heat that the bridge could not be closed to allow motorists to continue in and out of the City. To attempt to cool the hot steel, city officials had to spray it with water from the Harlem River for several hours. It was "only" 95 degrees out on July 8th 2024. Which is certainly a hot summer day, but not entirely unusual during a Manhattan summer, where temperatures above 90 degrees can happen up to 10 days per month in the months of July and August.

Your Public Transportation & Trains

What if my bus line stops running? Or the cost of my ticket goes way up? What if my commuter rail line is crumbling? Or, just too crowded to ever get a seat during peak hours? What if that new rail tunnel never opens? Are we ever going to get more high-speed rail lines?

Millions of Americans rely on public transit to get around. In crowded urban areas, they can be the fastest and most comfortable way to ride to work. For the elderly and handicapped, they can be the safest and most reliable transportation available. For someone who doesn't have, can't afford, or simply prefers not to use a car, they provide a less-expensive option. And, for people commuting between cities, a train ride is often just as fast, and more comfortable and productive than taking an airplane.

DOT grants are very important sources of funding for public transportation systems like bus and train lines. The grants pay for infrastructure like bus and rail terminals, upgrades to equipment, and maintenance. Sometimes, they are obviously huge, like the $16 billion Gateway Tunnel project linking New York and New Jersey, some funding for which has been withheld by the administration even though a judge has ordered that the funds be released. Other times, they are smaller when taken alone but huge when looked at together, like the administration's recent threat to withhold transportation grants from cities that offer free buses. There are forty such cities.

What if my bus or train line shuts, or crumbles, down --- how will I get to school or my job?

If your bus or train line shuts down, your daily commute could become significantly more challenging, impacting your ability to get to school or work. The Federal Railway Administration (FRA) oversees Amtrak and provides crucial discretionary rail grants that fund urban commuter rail. However, these grants, including $13 billion allocated under the Infrastructure Improvement and Jobs Act (IIJA) for 2025, were frozen in early 2025. And as of February 2026, funding of more than $18 billion for rail infrastructure projects in both New York and Chicago was still being withheld. This means vital funding for improvements and maintenance of bus and train lines is no longer reliably available, increasing the risk of service reductions or complete shutdowns.

For the over 800,000 people who rely on Amtrak and commuter rail every weekday, these cuts could mean longer commutes, increased transportation costs, or even job insecurity.

What if we stop investing in high-speed trains—will we fall further behind other countries?

Yes, the U.S. risks falling further behind other countries in modern transportation infrastructure. High-speed rail projects in Texas and California have been paused due to cuts in rail infrastructure investment. While the U.S. has an extensive rail network - a significant amount of freight still travels by rail in our country - a lack of investment in high-speed passenger rail means we are not keeping pace with other developed nations that are actively expanding their high-speed networks. This could impact our global competitiveness, as efficient transportation systems are crucial for economic growth and connectivity.

Airports & Air Travel

What if my airport gets less funding - will it still be maintained? Will it be safe? What if my airport is suddenly closed - will I get reimbursed for my flight? How will I even get where I need to go? What if our small airport loses funding? What will happen to tourism in our town? How will we connect to major hubs? Will our mail still be delivered on time? What if TSA is privatized or there are fewer agents - will flying be safe?

In February of 2026, the City of El Paso woke up to the news that its airport and airspace were shut down and would remain so for ten days. Ten hours later, that closure was reversed. But it wasn't reversed fast enough to prevent people from realizing what the fallout of disruptions to airports and air travel could include - airlines scrambling to reschedule passengers, pilots, flight attendants, and planes, ground crews left without work, empty cabs, empty hotels, mail and cargo flights not arriving, and emergency medical evacuation flights delayed or denied.

The brief closure of the El Paso airport was not the only sign of uncertainty in the security of airports and air travel in the past year. The FAA lost several hundred probationary employees due to Department of Government Efficiency layoffs in early 2025, in spite of being chronically understaffed and without apparent consideration of the costs to train new probationary employees. During the government shutdown of 2025, air traffic controllers were required to work without pay, leading not only to stress and burnout, but also to controllers calling in sick and even resigning. And, as of the time of writing, we are headed into another partial government shutdown that will affect the paychecks of some TSA workers.

What if my airport loses funding—will it become unsafe?

While the overall FAA budget might see an increase, regulatory goals outlined in 'Project 2025' could lead to significant changes that impact airport safety and operations. The proposed privatization of air traffic control and relaxing restrictions on foreign investment in U.S. airlines and airports could have major safety implications. The immediate layoff of 400 air traffic controllers has already caused disarray at airports, suggesting that reduced funding or changes in oversight could compromise safety and potentially lead to airport shutdowns or reduced operational capacity.

If my airport loses funding—will it shut down?

The President's discretionary budget request called for severe cuts to the "Essential Air Service" program, which subsidizes 180 small rural airports in the US, enabling rural Americans to gain access to major hubs via connecting flights. The Essential Air Service also guarantees mail and cargo flights - giving rural areas access to goods they could not otherwise get. And by subsidizing the airports themselves, EAS also supports emergency services like medical evacuation flights. Though the subsequently passed budget bill did not explicitly mention the same cuts, cuts to EAS are highly likely in the future, considering the Department of Transportation's policy of prioritizing urban development over projects that are considered too small to have a macroeconomic impact.

What if air traffic control becomes privatized or contracts are shifted to new companies—will flying still be safe?

This is a major concern for many. The disarray already seen from initial layoffs of federal aviation administration employees suggests that such a transition could lead to significant disruptions and potentially compromise the safety of air travel. The privatization of air traffic control is a key regulatory goal in Project 2025 and was attempted during the first Trump administration. While proponents argue for increased efficiency, critics raise serious questions about safety. Air traffic control is a complex and critical system, and transferring it to private entities could introduce new risks related to profit motives, reduced oversight, and potential compromises in training or technology.

The budget act recently signed into law includes an increase in funding for the FAA, touted as funding for critical air traffic control upgrades and the hiring of Air Traffic Controllers. The Big Beautiful Bill Act allocates $12.5 billion to the modernization of Air Traffic Control. The administration has, since April, repeatedly teased the idea that the entire contract for Air Traffic Control will go to one company - considered an impossible task by industry experts. But, in December of 2025, the DOT awarded the multi-billion-dollar contract to the private company Peraton. Transportation Secretary Duffy has claimed that Air Traffic Control will be modernized within 3-4 years. Meanwhile, there is language in the DOT funding package passed in January 2026 to prevent any DOT funding from being used to facilitate the privatization of Air Traffic Control.

What if my flight gets canceled or delayed—will I get any compensation?

The current Department of Transportation (DOT) is abandoning rules that required airlines to be transparent about prices and imposed a requirement that they pay reparations to passengers affected by long delays. There is a push to cease enforcement of rules that require compensation when flights are delayed by three or more hours. This means that if your flight is significantly delayed or canceled, you may not receive any compensation, leaving you to bear unexpected costs like accommodation or alternative travel arrangements. Meanwhile, rules that once required airlines to disclose additional fees - like baggage fees - upfront are being abandoned.

Emergencies & Economic Impact

Our roads, bridges, railway lines, and air travel interconnectivity are about much more than mere convenience. Modern infrastructure helps keep us safe and is foundational to all of our economic activities. If roads and bridges are old, weakened, riddled with frost heaves, and dotted with potholes, they're dangerous even on a beautiful day. If severe weather strikes, they risk crumbling altogether, leaving communities disconnected and costing a lot to replace and repair. And, what happens when fewer people can reach a town or city? In the first place, it takes longer and costs even more for emergency crews to arrive. In the long term, poorly connected transit takes a big economic toll. People cease visiting. It becomes harder and more costly to move goods and services in and out.

What if a hurricane or wildfire hits—will emergency crews be able to reach us?

Government budget cuts and policy changes are leading to less investment in resilient infrastructure and a focus on projects with a "macroeconomic impact," often neglecting rural areas. If roads are not built or maintained to withstand natural disasters like hurricanes or wildfires, they can become impassable, delaying or preventing emergency responders from reaching affected communities. When disasters strike, and the national highway system can't move people or supplies where they're needed most, communities on the margins are left even more vulnerable.

What if I live in a rural area—will first responders still get to me in time?

Reaching you in time will likely become more challenging for first responders. The new policies favor large-scale projects that promise macroeconomic returns, often sidelining rural communities in the process. As a result, critical infrastructure in these areas, which are vital for emergency services, risks being neglected or left behind. On top of that, restrictions on funding for equity-focused initiatives may further limit investment where it's needed most. These restrictions will deepen already stark disparities in access to life-saving emergency resources.

What if fewer people can travel to my town—what happens to our local economy?

When people can't get to your town, your economy feels it. For towns that depend on tourism or outside visitors, reduced access can mean fewer customers, declining business revenues, job losses, and shrinking public services. Over time, this disinvestment threatens not just local economies but the long-term sustainability of entire communities.

What if trucking slows down—will the price of groceries go up?

When transportation struggles, your grocery bill often feels the impact. Trucks are the backbone of how products get to stores all across the country. When roads aren't properly maintained or when new tolls and taxes make trucking more expensive, the whole supply chain slows down. This means trucks take longer to deliver goods, and the cost to move them rises. Unfortunately, those extra costs don't just disappear; they usually show up as higher prices at the checkout counter.

Pollution and Environmental Impact

What if there's a busy highway through my neighborhood, will our air quality get worse? Would it make a difference if my neighborhood had more parks and green spaces? What if my neighborhood becomes more industrialized, would it even be safe for my kids to live here in the future? I own an electric car, how am I going to charge it if there are fewer charging stations?

Getting around is one of those necessary human activities that takes a big toll on our environment. Vehicle emissions contribute to poor air quality, making it especially bad in high-traffic and urban areas. And road run-off is one of the leading causes of pollution in our waterways. In the past, the EPA and the DOT have worked together to both maximise our transportation options and minimize its environmental cost. Regulations raised fuel efficiency standards for cars. (Which also lowered the cost of ownership of cars.) Federal funds were dedicated to building a network of electric-vehicle charging stations under the NEVI program. City buses were being upgraded to the most fuel-efficient vehicles available. But a lot of this is changing under the current administration. In February 2026, the EPA announced its rescission of the

"Endangerment Finding", which was the science-based determination that greenhouse gases are harmful to human health. With that action, the EPA essentially gave up its own power to regulate emissions from not only motor vehicles, but also factories, power plants, and other emission-generating industries.

What if transportation cuts mean more pollution in my neighborhood?

If funding disappears and regulations are overturned or not enforced, pollution levels in your neighborhood could rise, possibly a lot. The current direction signals a move away from environmental reviews, sustainable infrastructure, and strict emissions standards. Without the input of the Environmental Protection Agency (EPA), the Department of Transportation might focus more on cutting costs or helping the auto industry, and less on keeping the air clean, leading to weaker rules on emissions. The EPA brings the scientific expertise needed to limit vehicle pollution, so when it's sidelined, standards can shift to favor industry interests over public health. That means dirtier air, more polluted runoff, and a real risk to the health of your local environment.

What if green spaces, walkable streets, or biking paths aren't built in my city?

Then we lose more than just aesthetics—we lose access, health, and safety. Equity-driven transportation projects are essential because they ensure that all communities, not just wealthy or well-connected ones, have safe ways to get around. Without these projects, many neighborhoods miss out on basic infrastructure like sidewalks, crosswalks, bike lanes, and public transit. As a result, people have fewer safe routes to reach jobs, schools, healthcare, and grocery stores. Car dependence increases, traffic gets worse, and air pollution rises. When investment in these communities stops, it makes cities harder to live in for everyone.

What if we stop investing in cleaner fuel --- will my kids breathe dirtier air?

Cleaner fuels and stronger emissions standards are critical because they reduce harmful pollutants released into the air. However, recent policy changes include relaxing fuel efficiency rules for planes and cutting back on investments in sustainable aviation fuels. These changes increase toxic emissions like nitrogen oxides and particulate matter. At the same time, vehicle emissions standards are also being cut, and programs like NEVI, the national electric vehicle charging initiative, which help promote cleaner electric cars, are being abandoned or stalled. This shift away from cleaner transportation fuels means more pollution in the air, which worsens respiratory problems like asthma and bronchitis, especially for children whose lungs are still developing.

What if electric vehicle charging stations disappear—how do I charge my car?

The National Electric Vehicle Infrastructure (NEVI) program was created to build a network of thousands of public EV charging stations across the country, supporting the rapid growth of electric vehicles, which are projected to make up over 50% of new car sales by 2030. However, funding for NEVI has been frozen and is currently tied up in litigation, putting these critical infrastructure plans at risk. Without widespread, accessible public charging, EV owners may face limited charging options, especially those without home chargers. This could slow EV adoption and increase reliance on gasoline vehicles, which would undermine emissions reduction goals.

Bottom Line

Modernized, safe, affordable, and clean transportation networks are a necessity. Our massive system of roads, railways, and airports is essential to our economy and to communities in every corner of the country. They facilitate the movement of people - to work, to schools, to shopping, to visiting one another - the movement of goods from where they are produced or where they arrive to the customers who need them - the movement of equipment and supplies necessary for emergency services and production. Disruption to our transportation networks disrupts lives, governments, and businesses. The importance of this network should make it clear that investments in its resilience are a wiser choice than responding to damage only after the fact.

CHAPTER 4
YOUR EDUCATION: SCHOOL DAYS AND STUDENT LOANS

PUBLIC SCHOOLS, COLLEGE AID, PELL GRANTS, STUDENT LOANS, RESEARCH FUNDING

Education is part of nearly every American's life, from preschool to college to job training. It affects not only your job opportunities, but also how you experience the world. School is where people discover their interests and their strengths, where they learn songs, poems, and stories that they never forget, and where they build friendships that last a lifetime. Government support is necessary in making education more affordable and accessible through public schools, financial aid, student loans, and research funding. When education budgets get slashed, the young people who miss out will feel it for life. And, ultimately, it will cost our entire society if more people grow up with limited skills and opportunities in the workforce.

What if I can't afford childcare even with my full-time job?

What if there's no one in my family who has time to read and play with my toddler? Does my kid have special needs, or is he just a normal four-year-old? We are teenage parents who love our kid - can someone help us learn the best ways to keep her safe and healthy?

The itsy-bitsy spider went up the water spout... You probably know the rest. You may have sung that song in preschool, sitting in a circle where everyone used their hands to mimic the spider climbing. It's not the height of intellectual and motor skills development, but it is an important step along the way. Pre-schools fill so many needs in our communities... They are safe child-care that working parents need for their kids, but that's not all. They're also among the first places where kids spend time in groups of their peers - learning social skills and playing cooperatively. They're where kids practice letters and numbers and learn the days of the week and the months of the year. They're places that provide fun, support, and structure for young kids, not only keeping them safe all day, but also giving the learning boost that sticks with them as they grow and move on to kindergarten, grade school, and beyond.

What if my child's preschool shut down —where would they go?

Preschool is more than early education. It supports child development and helps parents stay in the workforce. But when funding is cut or policies shift, programs can disappear, leaving families with few affordable alternatives.

One of the most vital pre-school programs at risk is Head Start. Head Start is a federally-funded preschool program serving over 800,000 children from low-income families and supports around 250,000 jobs nationwide. It provides early learning, meals, disability services, and family support to children, including vulnerable children who are in foster care, children with disabilities, and those from families experiencing homelessness. And, for many working parents, Head Start is not just a preschool; it's the foundation that makes employment possible.

Though Head Start funding survived recent federal budget negotiations, remaining at the 2024 funding level, serious threats remain. A previously leaked draft budget proposed eliminating the program entirely, and "Project 2025" openly calls for its shutdown. In the meantime, a federal funding freeze has already left the program about $1 billion short. Five of its 12 regional administrative offices remain closed, and many states have begun consolidating Head Start centers to cope with staffing and resource shortfalls. So far, there is no indication that the closed offices will reopen.

Most recently, a new rule excludes "undocumented immigrants" from accessing Head Start services. This has created confusion and fear, as the term "undocumented" has become increasingly unclear. In some cases, immigrants are being detained when showing up for court appointments to update or obtain legal documents. For Latino families, who make up more than half of Head Start's enrollment, this shift will have devastating effects. Even 100% percent American Latino families may now fear immigration raids on preschools, and be unwilling to enroll their children. The result is both a silent dismantling of the program from within, shrinking access and undermining trust, and a terrible loss for hundreds of thousands of children and their families.

What if my child needs extra help—who steps in if Head Start is gone?

Head Start doesn't only serve children from low-income families. It plays a critical role in supporting kids who face additional challenges, such as developmental delays, disabilities, unstable housing, or involvement in the foster care system. The program is federally required to reserve at least 10% of its enrollment for children with disabilities. It also offers tailored support services like speech therapy, behavioral health care, and individualized education plans. Head Start provides wraparound services like health screenings, meals, and family counseling that many other preschool options don't offer.

Not many other preschools can provide this level of support. Private preschools often lack the resources or expertise to meet these needs. And their costs, typically $10,000 to $15,000 per year, put private preschool out of reach for many families. Public Pre-K programs may offer some services and are free or low-cost in many areas, but access is uneven, and spots are limited, especially for children with special needs. Early Intervention programs provide therapies for children with disabilities, but serve a narrower group and don't replace Head Start's broader support for low-income families. Informal or family-based care lacks structured education and specialized services, and can place extra burdens on caregivers.

What would losing Head Start mean for my community?

Head Start doesn't just serve children—it supports an entire network of jobs. The program employs about 250,000 people nationwide, not only in classrooms but in food delivery, transportation, building maintenance, supply management, and family support services. These are local jobs that strengthen communities and keep dollars circulating in local economies. The ripple effects of closing Head Start would be felt in local economies, classrooms, and day-to-day lives across the country.

How will my kids eat lunch if the school lunch program is cut?

What if the price of school lunch goes way up, and our family can't afford it? What if there are fewer healthy options available for kids who eat school lunch? If I lose my SNAP benefits, will my kids also lose their access to school lunch? Our school used to serve food bought from farms in our own state - they even organized a field trip to that farm - what happened to that program?

Since 1946, the National School Lunch Program has helped schools provide free or low-cost lunches to students in need. Today, it serves over 28 million children each day across 94,000 schools—and for millions of those kids, it's one of the only meals they'll eat all day. SNAP cuts mean fewer families will qualify automatically for school lunches—putting more kids at risk of hunger during the school day, which can affect focus, learning, and health. And, looming Department of Education cuts will force schools into very tough decisions, including what could be for school lunch and who qualifies for it.

What if my child lost access to free lunch—would they go hungry?

Nearly 1 in 8 children in the U.S. live in food-insecure households. For many of these students, school-provided meals aren't just helpful, they're essential. According to the USDA, about 75% of lunches served through the national school lunch program are free or reduced-price, indicating just how many children rely on this support daily. The Cuts to SNAP made through the Big Beautiful Bill Act will make it harder for families to automatically qualify for free school meals. These cuts mean more kids falling through the cracks, missing meals, and going hungry during the school day.

For some kids, losing access to school lunch could mean missing their only guaranteed meal of the day. And hunger doesn't just affect the stomach. It shows up in the classroom—making it harder for kids to focus, stay engaged, or keep up academically. Teachers see it every day. In one national survey, 80% of educators said hunger hurts students' concentration, and over 75% reported a direct drop in academic performance. Children in food-insecure households are also 50% more likely to repeat a grade and 30% less likely to reach reading and math benchmarks. Hunger doesn't just follow a child to school—it follows them for life.

What if my school couldn't afford to serve meals at all?

Even if the National School Lunch Program continues, deep education budget cuts could force schools—especially in low-income districts—to reduce or eliminate meal services due to lack of staffing, kitchen resources, or operating funds. States that take in more state and local taxes might be able to continue the program, but districts that rely heavily on federal funds will be forced to make tough decisions, including which, if any, meals to provide. For millions of students, school lunch is the most reliable source of daily nutrition. Without funding to run these programs, children could face hunger, not because the program doesn't exist, but because their school can't afford to serve the food.

What if cuts hurt both kids and local farmers?

Programs like "Local Food for Schools" not only fed kids but supported local farmers by purchasing their food. Past cuts to these programs have already reduced funding by $1 billion. More cuts would mean fewer fresh, local meals for students and less income for small farmers. This hurts communities on both ends and takes away a great educational opportunity for kids - about farms, about their town, about nutrition - all the same time.

What does the Department of Education actually do anyway?

If the Department of Education closes, how will our town fund public schools? If people get vouchers that they can use at any school they want, would there still be public schools? How would my special-needs child get an education if the Department of Education shuts down? We are Jehovah's Witnesses, will there be a school that respects our choice of religion, or will our kids be picked on at school?

The Department of Education does more than hand out money to public schools. It supports K–12 schools, funds special education programs, enforces civil rights laws, manages student loans, and helps train teachers. Without it, many of those functions would be scattered across other federal agencies or transferred to the states, which would have wildly different capacities and priorities.

In March of 2025, the President signed an executive order to dismantle most of the Department of Education. Even though the legality of the order - whether or not the President can unilaterally shut down a government agency created by Congress - is still being litigated, the Supreme Court has allowed the administration to proceed with budget cuts and layoffs in the meantime, leaving the Department of Education, and thousands of public schools in very uncertain condition. Should they order those new textbooks for next year? Will the teachers be getting their scheduled training? Will standardized tests still be given? Will there be enough money for the soccer field, art program, after-school class, sets for the school play, tools for the shop class? No doubt, school administrators and teachers have just as many questions and concerns as the rest of us.

What happens to schools if the Department of Education shuts down?

If the Department of Education shuts down, the ripple effects on schools would be immediate and far-reaching. Schools in wealthier towns and wealthier states may be able to make up the difference in funding. But for districts that rely heavily on federal aid, cuts to it could be devastating. In Detroit, for example, nearly half of school funding — 47% — comes from Washington. Compare that to New York State, where only 7% of K–12 education is federally funded, and you see the problem: the more you depend on federal dollars, the steeper the cliff. Losing that support could mean larger class sizes, fewer teachers, cuts to after-school programs, outdated textbooks, and the collapse of services for English learners or students with disabilities.

In short, shutting down the Department of Education would cut off a critical lifeline from the country's most vulnerable schools. Some districts would scramble to fill the gap; others simply couldn't. The result would be a deeper divide between well-resourced communities and those already fighting to keep the lights on.

What if my child has a disability—will they still get support?

Federal law guarantees that students with disabilities are entitled to a free and appropriate public education. The Department of Education plays a central role in making sure that promise is kept — it enforces the Individuals with Disabilities Education Act (IDEA), distributes billions in special education funding to states, and investigates when districts fail to meet students' needs.

Without the federal government enforcing IDEA and supplying dedicated funding, support for students with disabilities would vary widely. In well-resourced states or districts, students might continue receiving most services. In poorer or underfunded areas, students could face delays, reductions, or complete gaps in critical support. Families would have to fight harder, seek outside providers, or even move to a different district or state to ensure their children receive legally-guaranteed education services.

What if my child is bullied—who protects my child?

The Department of Education enforces civil rights laws in schools, such as Title VI and Title IX, which protect students from discrimination based on race, gender, religion, or disability. These laws give families ways to challenge bullying and ensure a safe and fair learning environment.

If the Department of Education were eliminated, these protections could weaken, leaving students with fewer options to address harassment or discrimination, and potentially allowing unsafe or unfair practices to continue unchecked.

What about the education vouchers?

Would we be able to use them to get the same or better education? Would kids have the same protections in private schools?

Federal funds that currently support public schools and uphold students' rights could be redirected to private school voucher programs, which provide public money for students to attend private schools, including religious institutions. Private schools receiving these funds are not always required to follow the same civil rights protections as public schools, which could leave students more vulnerable to discrimination.

Redirecting funds in this way could also drain resources from public schools, leading to cuts in programs that support all students, including those with disabilities. Vouchers might disproportionately benefit families who already have options for private education, widening the gap between well-resourced students and those in underfunded districts.

Eliminating the Department of Education could both reduce federal protections against bullying and discrimination and shift public dollars to schools where equal treatment is not guaranteed, leaving many students more exposed and underserved.

What if my school can't afford updated books or trained teachers?

In 2024, the Department of Education distributed $150 billion in grants to help schools cover essential needs, including hiring teachers, paying for training, and buying up-to-date textbooks. If the department is eliminated, much of this funding could be shifted into block grants — a type of funding that gives states a lump sum of money with fewer federal rules about how it must be spent. While block grants give states more flexibility, they also mean less oversight to ensure the money reaches classrooms and supports students directly. Some states might choose to divert the funds elsewhere, leaving schools short on teachers, training, and essential materials.

In practical terms, this could mean classrooms where teachers are stretched thin because schools don't have enough money to hire or retain staff. Schools might have to combine classes, increase student-to-teacher ratios, or cut specialized programs like art, music, or tutoring. Textbooks, technology, and other learning materials could become outdated or insufficient, making it harder for students to keep up with curriculum standards. Schools in wealthier districts might be able to make up the difference with local taxes, but underfunded districts wouldn't have that option, leaving students there at a significant disadvantage. Without consistent federal support, the quality of education a child receives could vary dramatically depending on where they live.

What if education funding depends on my zip code—is that fair?

Inequalities between districts already exist, but federal funding helps close the gap. Federal dollars provide extra support to schools in poorer areas for teachers, textbooks, special programs, and other resources that wealthier districts can often fund on their own. If these funds are handed over to states with fewer rules, schools in wealthy areas could maintain or even expand programs using local taxes, while schools in low-income areas might face cuts, larger class sizes, fewer qualified teachers, outdated materials, and reduced support services. In practice, this would make the quality of a child's education even more dependent on their zip code, intensifying the inequities that persist.

Over time, these differences would accumulate: students in underfunded schools could fall further behind in reading and math, miss out on extracurricular and enrichment opportunities, and experience lower graduation rates. This would deepen the cycle where children in low-income areas are denied the same educational foundation as their wealthier peers, limiting their future opportunities for college, careers, and upward mobility — all because of the circumstances of their location, not their ability or effort.

What if my school starts discriminating —who stops it?

The Department of Education doesn't just respond to individual complaints; it monitors schools to ensure they follow federal civil rights laws like Title VI and Title IX. These laws prevent discrimination in how students are admitted, disciplined, or given access to programs and resources. If the department is eliminated, that monitoring and enforcement largely disappear. Schools could develop policies or practices that systematically favor some students over others — for example, steering certain racial or economic groups into lower-level classes, disproportionately suspending students from marginalized backgrounds, or limiting access to advanced coursework or extracurricular programs.

Without federal oversight, state and local authorities would have to enforce these laws, but not all states have the resources, expertise, or political will to do so consistently. Over time, this could create deeply entrenched patterns of inequality that are much harder to undo. Students in underfunded or poorly monitored districts will face more structural barriers to achievement.

What if my public school starts pushing religion—do I have a say?

The Department of Education plays an important role in ensuring that public schools respect the separation of church and state. It monitors schools and enforces federal rules that prevent government-funded schools from promoting or favoring religious beliefs. If the department is eliminated, this oversight disappears, leaving schools with much more leeway to introduce religious instruction, activities, or messaging in ways that could pressure students or influence classroom content.

Without federal scrutiny, the extent and impact of religious influence could vary widely between districts. Some schools might subtly favor certain faiths in their curricula or extracurricular programs, while others could actively encourage participation in religious rituals or teachings. Families who do not share those beliefs may have little recourse, particularly in underfunded districts where alternative public options are limited. Over time, this could create environments in which students feel coerced or excluded because of their personal beliefs, and where educational content is shaped by ideology rather than objective learning standards. In short, eliminating the Department of Education could shift public schools from neutral spaces for learning to places where religion influences both curriculum and culture, undermining parents' and students' ability to ensure a secular, inclusive education.

What if we can't afford to send our kids to college?

Does that mean they just can't go? Our daughter wants to be a nurse, but the education and training would cost a lot in relation to what she would be able to get paid doing the job. Should she still do it? What's going to happen to our State school if both student loans and research grants are cut? Will it still be able to offer in-state tuition to our kids? Our son is working while in college, but he still needs his grants and loans to make ends meet. How will the changes to these programs affect him? I want to go to college, but I'm worried that I won't be able to pay back the loans...

People want their children to go to college for a lot of reasons. Yes, the degree matters for future opportunities. But it's not just a trade of four years and lots of money for a piece of paper that helps you land a job. College is a gateway to opportunity. It is where young people discover their true skills and interests and have their first opportunity to apply and specialize in them. College is where young engineers hone their skills with expert guidance, where aspiring writers collaborate with published authors, and where doors are opened to opportunities for scientific exploration. The personal and professional relationships students form in college can last a lifetime. And once the door to advanced education is open, some people choose to specialize even further, continuing on to earn the advanced degrees required to become, for example, a doctor.

Yes, many of us want to go to college for a lot of reasons. But college is expensive. Families have a hard time cobbling together the funds needed for college. Many start saving for college the moment a child is born. Others do not have the income needed to do that while working and paying all of the other bills that come up along the way. To try to make college education accessible, the government has a series of grant and loan programs:

- **Pell Grants** provide financial support for education for young people who have the most financial need. These do not have to be paid back.

- **Subsidized Student Loans** are loans that do not accrue interest while students are still in school.
- **Repayment plans and forbearance options** help keep graduates' loan repayment amounts reasonable in relation to their post-graduation income and can allow people to pause payments during periods of hardship.
- **Public Interest Student Loan Forgiveness** makes it possible for more people to pursue careers like nursing and teaching, which are important to communities but don't pay as much as other jobs.

What if my family can't afford college—does my kid miss out?

College in the U.S. is the most expensive in the world, and about 70% of students graduate with debt. Changes under the Trump administration could make paying for college even harder. New rules limit how much students are allowed to borrow, potentially putting the best college or graduate program for your kid's interests and skills out of reach. Meanwhile, subsidized federal student loans help students pay for tuition and living expenses while they are in school without charging interest until after graduation, making it more manageable to afford college. Ending these loans - as was attempted in early versions of the Big Beautiful Bill Act - would mean students start accruing interest as soon as the loan is disbursed, even while attending classes, causing total debt to grow faster.

In practical terms, these changes would push higher education out of reach for many students who rely on federal loans, making it harder to access the degrees and opportunities that lead to better-paying jobs and upward mobility.

What if my kid wants to be a teacher or nurse—but can't afford the debt?

The Public Service Loan Forgiveness (PSLF) program helps students who enter public service careers, such as teaching, nursing, social work, or government jobs, by forgiving the remaining balance on their federal student loans after they make 10 years of qualifying payments. This program makes it possible for people to choose lower-paying public service careers without being crushed by student debt. Many graduates, now professionals, rely on the program and have made payments in reliance on the program for several years. Not only would ending or severely eroding PSLF cut off the supply of public service workers at the source, it would also throw the lives of all of those graduates into disarray.

The executive branch is seeking to cut back on this loan forgiveness program in a number of ways, including redefining which professions are eligible for the program and which types of organizations a public service professional can work for and still be eligible for the program. In an executive order issued in March 2025, the President made it clear he wants certain non-profit workers to be ineligible for the program.

Meanwhile, the caps on graduate school borrowing in the big beautiful bill act mean that the loans of people who need an advanced degree for their public service job, like nurse practitioners, will not be entirely eligible for PSLF. To cover the full cost of the degree, an aspiring nurse practitioner might even have to take out high-interest private loans, which would not only not be eligible for forgiveness after years of service but would be more expensive to pay off.

With the cuts to PSLF that have already happened, and those that may still be to come, students who wanted to dedicate their professional lives to serving their communities may not be able to. Graduates might be forced to take higher-paying private-sector jobs instead of pursuing the careers that they're truly passionate about. The result could be serious work-force shortages in critical areas like schools, hospitals, and social work, leaving communities without enough teachers, nurses, and other essential professionals — all because student debt makes these careers financially unviable for many young people.

What if my kid's college can't survive the budget cuts?

Many colleges depend on federal funding, including grants and student loans, to cover operating costs like salaries for faculty and staff, maintenance of facilities, and academic programs. If the federal budget for education is cut or funding is eliminated, colleges could face serious financial shortfalls. To cope, they might be forced to lay off professors and staff, reduce course offerings, cut extracurricular programs, or even close entire departments or campuses. In extreme cases, some colleges could shut down entirely. For students, this would mean losing access to the school they enrolled in, along with the time, money, and effort they have already invested. Ultimately, budget cuts could destabilize the higher education system, leaving students with fewer options and forcing many to reconsider whether completing college is even possible or worth it.

Bottom Line

The truth is, your child's education—what they learn, how they're supported, and what opportunities they have—depends on a web of public systems most of us rarely see. Cuts to these systems don't just "reduce spending." They close doors. They widen gaps. And they make your child's future more dependent on luck, location, and income than ability.

If preschool disappears… if schools lose funding… if protections weaken… if college becomes unaffordable…

You'll find out just how much education mattered—and how much of it depended on what we chose to support.

CHAPTER 5
THE FOOD ON YOUR FORK

USDA, FDA, FARM SUBSIDIES, SNAP

Food should be simple: you go to the grocery or market, grab what you need, and cook dinner. Sometimes you're eating special foods reserved for holidays and celebrations. Other times, you're grabbing a quick bite to stave off hunger while charging through a busy day. While there's no arguing that too many of us are worried about how much those trips to the store cost these days, we are fortunate that most of us are not worried that the food we eat will make us sick.

Every bite you take is shaped by an enormous, mostly invisible system of protections and policies. There are safety checks that keep salmonella out of your chicken. There are farm subsidies that determine whether apples or potato chips are cheaper. And, there are trade agreements that determine whether there are avocados on the shelf. Government programs touch your plate every single day.

When those programs are cut, the effects don't just play out in Washington — they land right at your dinner table. They decide whether your grocery bill is affordable, whether your kids get a hot meal at school, and whether you can trust the food in your fridge. This chapter looks at what happens when those protections weaken — not in abstract policy terms, but in real life, for families trying to eat and stay healthy.

What if I don't know which foods are safe to eat?

How does a fruit or vegetable grown in another state, or even country, stay fresh and clean all the way to my local store? Which kind of lettuce was it that made people sick? Who handled this steak all the way between the ranch and the refrigerator aisle? I heard that someone in another state got sick from peanut butter. Is the peanut butter in my state safe to eat? How did this listeria outbreak happen, and which foods are safe? We have frozen meals that we bought months before the recall notice, are they safe to eat?

Most of us assume the food on our plate is safe — that our chicken is free of salmonella, our lettuce is clean, and that we won't end up in the ER after eating cold cuts from the deli. That confidence doesn't come from luck. It comes from layers of protection that government agencies provide. The

Food and Drug Administration (FDA), the Department of Agriculture (USDA), and the Centers for Disease Control and Prevention (CDC) work together and separately to create a vast safety net that keeps most of our food safe, and teaches us how to protect ourselves if something dangerous in food does make it to the stores.

- **The FDA** requires farms and factories to have safety plans, conducts inspections, and issues recalls when something goes wrong.
- **The USDA's Food Safety and Inspection Service** has inspectors inside meat, poultry, and egg plants to make sure contamination doesn't slip by.
- **The CDC** connects the dots when people across different states get sick and warns the public when there's an outbreak.

You can think of it as a much larger version of the way you handle food yourself. You put your perishable items in the fridge. You peel your carrots. You discard milk that's been around too long. You wash your hands and wipe your counters after cooking. You don't combine ingredients that spoil each other. You do all of this to keep your food both tasty and safe to eat. The food safety system works to make sure that the same food is safe when you buy it. And that often means paying attention to it during the many months and miles it takes before it ever reaches your store. Food safety involves things like -

- Making sure that vegetables are watered with clean water
- Making sure that the food animals are fed is safe
- Making sure that the fertilizers and pest-control products aren't toxic
- Making sure that food products are always stored at safe temperatures everywhere along the long line from the farm to your grocery store shelf
- Making sure there's no stagnant water pooling in a meat processing plant
- Making sure that shipping containers are free of parasites and vermin
- Making sure that the expiration dates on foods are labeled
- And more... because food safety in a country as large as ours and in a world where food products are shipped from just about everywhere is a very big undertaking.

These services matter much more than most of us realize. Even with these protections in place, 48 million Americans still get sick from foodborne illness every year. That's one in seven of us. About 128,000 end up in the hospital, and 3,000 die. Right now, with these numbers of illnesses, we are still ranked as having one of the safest food supplies in the world. Without these agencies doing their work, the number of people getting sick from food would skyrocket.

Cuts to food safety programs across agencies are pulling people off the front lines, pausing or ending important food safety programs, and causing delays and miscommunications of threats to food safety. More than 4,000 FDA employees have been laid off or have accepted deferred resignation offers. The USDA lost more than 15,000 workers to deferred resignations, including hundreds of food safety and inspection service workers. And, at least 600 outbreak experts have lost jobs at the CDC. On top of this loss of expertise, food safety regulations have also been thrown into disarray with the administration demanding "limited enforcement" of rules such as those overseeing the traceability of produce, pet food labeling guidelines, and listeria in ready-to-eat foods.

What does this mean in everyday life?

It means fewer inspectors standing inside processing plants.

Fewer tests run on food before it ships.

Slower recalls when contamination is detected.

And less information for doctors and families trying to decide whether a stomachache is just bad luck—or something more serious.

Can't the states just take over food inspection services?

Right now, 21 states don't even have their own certified meat inspection programs, and the USDA has already lost thousands of workers. What does that mean? It means there are fewer trained inspectors standing inside slaughterhouses and processing plants, checking food before it ever reaches your grocery store.

The way it works now, every single day a meat processing plant operates, federal inspectors are physically present. They examine animals before and after slaughter, make sure equipment and facilities are clean, and watch for visible signs of contamination or disease. They also take samples for lab testing to catch bacteria like Salmonella, E. coli, or Listeria. By law, meat and poultry can't cross state lines without passing either a federal inspection or an inspection that is equally rigorous by a state inspection service that is certified by the federal government.

Unfortunately, it can be challenging to hold state inspection agencies to the same standard as the well-resourced federal agency. They may not have the same resources and expertise as the USDA. And, it's also certainly a lot to ask of the USDA to complete oversight of state agencies in addition to the inspection work they already do.

We've recently seen the kind of widespread

damage that can happen when there are major failures in the food safety system:

In 2024, contaminated deli meat from a Boar's Head plant killed 10 people and sickened 61 more across 19 states. The plant was inspected by a state-run, but federally-certified, inspection service, and the contamination went unnoticed (or unchecked). The result was not just tragic for the families who lost loved ones. Small businesses across the country — delis, corner markets, cafes, and just about anyplace that sold sandwiches — lost money when customers stopped trusting anything with the Boar's Head label.

For a regular person, food safety isn't about "policy." It's about whether you can trust the turkey sandwich you buy at lunch. It's about whether you feel safe handing your kid a hot dog at a baseball game. And it's about whether small businesses in your community can survive when people stop trusting the food supply. Without strong federal food safety systems, every meal becomes a gamble — and the cost of getting it wrong is measured in lives, livelihoods, and trust.

What about the SNAP Cuts? Will families really go hungry?

How many people does SNAP reach anyway? Does SNAP just hand out money to people? SNAP benefits are so small anyway, don't recipients have to have other money for food? Will losing SNAP benefits affect people's eligibility for other benefits programs like school lunches or home-heating assistance? How does it affect our town if people who live here lose their SNAP benefits?

How many people rely on SNAP?

Food insecurity is a real problem in our country. Tens of millions of us don't know where our next meal is coming from. SNAP, often called food stamps, is one of the quiet workhorses of American life. Right now, it helps about 42 million people — that's 12% of the population — put groceries on the table. And even with SNAP, food insecurity is widespread. More than 13% of Americans don't know where their next meal is coming from. Those aren't just numbers on the page — it's the parent skipping dinner so their kids can eat, or the elderly neighbor cutting her pills in half because she had to choose between buying medicine or food.

The cuts to SNAP put through in the Big Beautiful Bill Act are the steepest cuts in the program's history - 187 billion by 2034. They will take billions of *meals off tables every year.* These cuts shrink SNAP so much that more than half of today's recipients could lose their benefits by 2034. Imagine what that looks like in real life: grocery carts with fewer fresh foods, kids going to bed hungry, parents relying on food banks already stretched thin. Tens of millions more families would have to start making impossible choices — rent or groceries, gas for work, or dinner for the family.

How do SNAP benefits work? Can people just keep the money and not buy food? What good does SNAP actually do for our town?

SNAP benefits are not redeemable for cash. SNAP recipients can only use the benefits at certified retailers. The money is transferred directly to the retailers. This means both that SNAP recipients always use the benefits to buy food *and* that SNAP benefits support retailers and jobs. Estimates from the Commonwealth Fund indicate that SNAP cuts alone could cost the economy more than 150,000 jobs in food service, trucking, retail, and agriculture. And, of course, communities that lose jobs also lose the income taxes that people who had those jobs once paid, putting even more people into economic hardship.

How is SNAP being cut?

SNAP cuts are happening in a lot of ways that will make it harder to qualify, easier to lose eligibility, and less possible to afford healthy food, even for people who do qualify. Even though the majority of adult SNAP recipients already work full time - 40% of SNAP recipients are children - new work requirements will throw people off of SNAP by extending the work requirements to some of the most vulnerable people among us, such as homeless families, children aging out of foster care, and veterans. The cuts will also force states to cover a larger share of SNAP benefit funding, which could lead to gross disparities, with some states able to maintain benefits while others are forced to cut them much further. *And,* since the Big Beautiful Bill Act also restricts updates to the Thrifty Food Plan, which is how the amount of benefits needed to afford a healthy diet is determined, the benefits that people do manage to qualify for will continue to decrease in relation to the cost of healthy food.

Would losing SNAP benefits make it harder for our family to get other assistance that we need?

The ripple effects of losing SNAP benefits don't stop at the kitchen cabinets either. Because of the strict verification required to qualify for SNAP, having qualified for it can help families in need qualify faster for other forms of assistance. Many children qualify for free or reduced-price school lunches because their families receive SNAP. Those school lunches aren't just a bonus — for some kids, they're the only reliable meal they get all day. Families can also qualify faster for other assistance like the Low Income Home Energy Assistance Program (LIHEAP), which not only helps people keep their homes warm in winter, but can also enable them make healthier choices when it comes to using SNAP benefits - A bag of beans is a lot more nutritious and goes a lot further than a box of crackers. But, you have to be able to - and be able afford to - cook them.

For most of us, food is the most basic thing we expect in life. We assume the grocery store will be there when we need it, and our kids won't go hungry in a country as wealthy as the United States. But SNAP is what makes that possible for millions of families.

What if farm subsidies were unfairly weighted towards certain kinds of crops or inadequate to meet farmers' needs?

What is a farm subsidy anyway? What if I don't have the cash or credit to keep my farm running while we wait for the subsidies to arrive? What if we want to grow healthy food to sell directly in our own and nearby towns, will we qualify for subsidies?

At its core, a farm subsidy is money the government gives or guarantees to farmers to keep the food system stable. Farming is unpredictable — a drought, flood, or shifts in global crop prices can wipe out a farmer's income. Farming is also a business where a lot of investments have to be made upfront. Crops are planted and tended before they're harvested. Animals have to be raised. Subsidies act as a safety net so farmers don't go bankrupt every time something goes wrong.

They take a few different forms. Sometimes it's crop insurance, where the government helps cover losses if bad weather ruins a harvest. Sometimes it's disaster relief, like payments to farmers after a wildfire or flood. There are also price supports, which kick in if the market price of crops falls too low, so farmers can still afford to keep planting. There are (were) many cases in which the government even buys food directly from farmers — like milk, produce, or grains— to use in school lunch programs or food banks and, in the past, for distribution as international aid.

The idea is that if farmers know they won't lose everything in a bad year, they'll keep producing food steadily, and we as consumers will have consistent, affordable groceries. Without that safety net, farms would go under more easily, and food prices would swing wildly based on weather or global markets.

What is the situation like right now? Why do farms need subsidies if farm aid was already approved in the Big Beautiful Bill Act?

Right now, in spite of promises of increased aid for farmers, our farmers are facing a lot of uncertainty. So many things have changed. Direct purchase programs have been cut or cancelled entirely. Tariffs have driven up the costs of inputs and equipment that farmers rely on. Immigration policies have decreased the number of farm workers. And international trade disputes have left commodities farmers with far fewer guaranteed buyers for their crops. In January of 2026, a group of more than 50 agricultural and farming associations sent a letter to Congress warning of dire consequences for farmers if farm aid is not expedited. The number of Chapter 12 farm bankruptcies in 2025 was 46% higher than the year before, and that does not include insolvency at small family farms that are ineligible to file for Chapter 12.

Do farm subsidies help farmers of healthy foods and help make healthy foods more affordable?

Farm subsidies do help stabilize farmers and farming communities, but sometimes they're weighted in favor of some crops and not others. Right now, subsidies are weighted heavily toward big commodity crops like corn, wheat and soy. (Those are the ingredients that end up in animal feed, soda, and ultra-processed foods and/or get exported in massive quantities.) At the same time, support for "specialty crops", healthy food, like fruits, vegetables, and nuts is very low. The "Farmer Bridge Assistance Program" announced by the Department of Agriculture in December of 2025 to give emergency assistance to farmers reserves only $1 billion of it's $12 billion total for specialty crop farms.

What does the distinction between "specialty crops" and "row crops" in farm subsidies mean for you?

In simple terms, the food that's bad for you gets cheaper, while the food that's good for you gets more expensive. Apples, lettuce, and almonds could rise in price because small and mid-sized farmers won't have the same safety net to keep their crops affordable.

Meanwhile, soda, chips, and processed meat stay cheap because the base ingredients — corn syrup, soy oil, animal feed — are still heavily subsidized.

This doesn't just affect what people buy at the supermarket. Local farmers who grow produce for farmers' markets, CSAs, or small groceries could see their income shrink, forcing some out of business. When those farms close, communities lose not only fresh food but also jobs and local economic activity. You may find fewer healthy options at your store, or notice your favorite farm stand disappearing.

While farm subsidies might sound like an abstract budget line, they're actually one of the biggest forces shaping your plate. Eliminate or shift them, and you change what families can afford to eat, what kids get in their school lunches, and whether small farms in your community survive at all.

What if food imports got disrupted? What would be on store shelves?

Why worry about food imports? Aren't they just exotic foods and expensive spices? Where do most of our fruits and vegetables come from? If we have a trade dispute with Mexico, where will we get fruit in winter?

The "international foods" aisle at the grocery store might make you think those exotic foods are all there are to food imports, but the truth is that a huge part of the fruit and vegetable section is imported, too. 60% of all of our fresh fruit and almost 40% of our fresh vegetables are imported. About one out of every five bites of food you eat comes from another country. The U.S. imports roughly 20% of its food, and a lot of it comes from close trading partners like Mexico and Canada. There are lots of reasons for this. Some crops just grow better in the climates of other countries, and fish are more plentiful in some waters. In warmer climates, crops can be planted and harvested year-round. Food imports give us access to a year-round supply of fruits and vegetables that, in most of our territory, would only be available a few months a year. Many of the foods we take for granted aren't grown here in the quantities we need, or at all.

This system works fine when trade is smooth. But when conflicts heat up — tariffs, trade wars, political fights — food is often one of the first things to be disrupted. The U.S. already runs a food trade deficit with Mexico and Canada, which means we depend on them to keep store shelves stocked. If those trade relationships fray, prices on basics like produce and meat can jump overnight. If trade breaks down, the supply chain for those foods is disrupted. Trucks don't cross the border, ships don't unload, and grocery distributors can't restock. In some cases, foods could just vanish from stores for weeks or months. And if imports do start moving again, there's often a lag: it can take weeks for shipments to catch up, so shortages last longer than people expect.

For a regular person, that doesn't just mean higher grocery bills. It also means walking into the store and not finding the staples you're used to. Maybe the price of limes doubles, strawberries disappear, there's no vanilla extract for your cake, and no black beans for your salad. The price of coffee could rise to the stratosphere, and chocolate could become rare. Restaurants might pull certain items from the menu or raise prices to cover costs. Families who already live on tight food budgets will feel the squeeze the hardest, cutting back on fresh produce or protein because it's suddenly out of reach.

We've seen smaller versions of this before — like when supply chains froze during COVID, and people couldn't find eggs, flour, or baby formula. Outside of a pandemic, disruptions usually look different but have the same effect: one weak link in the chain can throw the whole system off. A labor strike, a factory fire, or contamination in a single large facility can create ripple effects that leave shelves empty nationwide. Because food distribution is so centralized, losing just one big processing plant or shipping hub can feel like pulling a key piece out of a Jenga tower — everything gets shakier, and shortages spread quickly.

Either way, the result is the same: the food exists somewhere, but it can't get to you. That's when you walk into a grocery store and see empty shelves where fresh produce or imported staples usually are — not because farmers stopped growing it, but because the system that moves food around the world broke down.

What if food prices keep rising — who feels it most?

Does it really matter if some food is expensive as long as some other food is still affordable? Isn't it just a matter of what you choose to buy at the store? What are the long term impacts of high food prices?

No one needs convincing that groceries cost more today than they used to. A gallon of milk that cost $3 a few years ago is now closer to $5. A pack of chicken breasts that used to be under $8 can easily top $12. But at the same time, a bag of chips is still around a dollar or two, and a two-liter soda often costs less than a bottle of water. Prices are still climbing, even if not as fast as during the big jumps in 2021 and 2022, and the foods going up the most are the ones we rely on for healthy meals.

When processed foods are so much less expensive than fresh and healthy foods, the gap matters. It matters because a family trying to stretch $40 at the store can buy enough pasta, boxed dinners, and snack foods to last for several days. But what if they wanted to eat a more balanced diet? The same $40 might only cover a couple of pounds of produce, some meat, and milk. The cost difference is the difference between filling a cart with food that's cheap but less nutritious, or buying a much smaller cart of healthier food that runs out faster. When money is tight, most families have no real choice: they go with the cheaper calories so there's enough to keep everyone fed.

Over time, this creates a divide in health outcomes. Households with less money eat more processed food because that's what they can afford. This leads to higher rates of obesity, diabetes, and heart disease in poorer communities. Those illnesses lead to more doctor visits, higher medical bills, and shorter life spans. In other words: today's expensive groceries become tomorrow's health crisis.

Meanwhile, wealthier families can absorb the higher prices. They might complain about spending more at the grocery store - they might even cut back in other places - but they can still put balanced meals on the table. The burden falls hardest on those who already struggle the most.

Bottom Line

The truth is, the food on your plate—what it costs, whether it's safe, and whether it's even there—depends on a system most of us never see. Cuts to that system don't just "reduce spending." They raise prices.

They increase risk. And they make something as basic as feeding your family less certain.

If inspectors disappear... if benefits shrink... if farms fail... if supply chains break...

You'll find out just how much your next meal depended on the things we're now cutting.

CHAPTER 6

YOUR SECURITY: SAFE AND SOUND (OR NOT?)

FIRE & POLICE FUNDING, FEMA, DISASTER PREPAREDNESS, NATIONAL GUARD

Security isn't just something you need in airports, power plants, oil refineries, and big cities. It's a vast nationwide - worldwide even - network of people and services that protect us from all kinds of possible harm. They do visible things, like drive fire trucks, and invisible things like track cyber threats. They work to prevent gun violence and drug overdoses. They fight wildfires and clear roads after storms. Some patrol the streets, others fold blankets in homeless shelters. And they are *all* part of organizations that protect our security. There are many federal and state agencies and nonprofit organizations whose focus is on protecting us. They provide the help that arrives if a fire breaks out, a storm hits, a crime happens, or a child goes missing.

People may expect these services to simply be there as part of the background of modern life. But they're far from automatic. They have been built over generations of constant public investment—staffing, training, equipment, planning, coordination. Work is done long before an emergency ever happens. When investment in that work is cut, redirected, or politicized, security may not disappear all at once. But it will fray. And when you need help most, you find out what's missing.

What if you weren't sure help would be there?

Where does all of this public safety money go? I thought my town was responsible for our police and fire departments? What if the whole town is blocked in after a storm, how will anyone get to us? What if a child is taken across state lines? What if a lot of people in town have become addicted to a new drug? Who runs the domestic abuse hotline?

Protecting security and public safety is very complex, as risks and threats to safety come in many forms. It's not always as visible as a destructive storm. Sometimes threats come in the form of dangerous addictions that make people desperate. Other times, a hacker threatens to drain hundreds of thousands of bank accounts. That is why billions of federal dollars flow every year to support public safety at the state, local, and tribal levels. That money doesn't just fund police departments. It supports:

- Firefighters and emergency medical responders
- Disaster preparation and recovery
- Search-and-rescue teams
- Victim support services
- Courts and corrections
- Substance abuse and mental health programs
- Violence prevention
- Training for first responders and public officials

Much of this funding moves through three main places:

- The Department of Justice
- The Department of Homeland Security, including the Federal Emergency Management Agency
- The Department of Defense, particularly for the National Guard

These systems are meant to work together. When one weakens, pressure shifts to the others. Right now, all of them are under strain, from direct budget cuts and from shifting priorities.

What if public safety funding could be turned on and off overnight?

Does it matter if there's less money this year if we already have a police force? What happens if the prison system in our state loses federal support? Someone is still tracking terror threats against our public infrastructure, right?

Funding for public safety has been thrown into disarray, and communities into uncertainty, as billions of dollars in public safety grants have been frozen or canceled. This has left states scrambling to fund public safety training and equipment, while the non-profits that work to save lives and assist the neediest among us don't know if they'll be able to afford to operate in the future.

Cuts to public safety grants and changes in public safety priorities are numerous. There have been hundreds of millions in funding cuts to violence prevention programs. There are ongoing threats and efforts to withhold funding from states that refuse to comply with federal immigration policy. Hundreds of millions in grants to public safety non-profits have been cancelled or withheld. These weren't hypothetical programs. They paid for:

- Police staffing and training
- Domestic violence shelters

- Addiction treatment
- Juvenile justice programs
- Victim services
- Data systems used to track crime and missing persons

Some states and cities lost funding with little notice. Others were warned their grants could disappear if they didn't comply with unrelated political demands. In Maine, the Department of Corrections was suddenly unsure whether it could operate from one day to the next after federal funds were frozen in a dispute unrelated to public safety. The message is clear: public safety funding is being used as leverage.

For communities, that kind of uncertainty is destabilizing. You can't plan staffing, training, or emergency response when your funding might vanish overnight. Security depends on predictability. Weaponized funding destroys it.

Meanwhile, Federal departments have cut ties with expert organizations that monitored extremist groups in the U.S. And offices within the State Department that worked to monitor and counter terrorism threats from abroad have been cut back.

What if a disaster hits?

Why is it that every time a storm hits, more and more of our infrastructure gets destroyed? What if our whole state is hit? How will state workers, trucks, and equipment get to us? This has happened before, why weren't we ready before the storm?

Storm preparedness and coordinated response are important to our security. To be safe, we need to keep roads open, we need utilities to function, and we need help lines to respond to calls. The safety net people rely on in natural disasters is layered. Local responders are first on the scene. State resources follow. And, federal support fills the gaps—especially when damage is widespread. That federal backstop matters more than most people realize.

In the first place, we want to be ready *before* disaster strikes. When it comes to natural disasters, being ready doesn't just mean having crews ready to clear roads; it means building and maintaining infrastructure that can withstand the weather. That was one of the goals of the Infrastructure Improvement and Jobs Act. But, in April 2025, FEMA eliminated the Building Resilient Infrastructure and Communities (BRIC) program entirely. That single decision cut off $880 million in grants for stronger infrastructure in 2025 and ended a program that had delivered $5 billion nationwide to help communities prepare for floods, fires, storms, and earthquakes *before* disasters happened.

At the same time, the Flood Mitigation Assistance program was eliminated, and the future of the

National Flood Insurance Program was thrown into uncertainty. These weren't emergency-response programs. They were prevention. Which means the damage doesn't show up immediately. It shows up later—when floods are worse, fires spread faster, and recovery costs skyrocket.

We saw exactly what that looks like in July 2025.

When the system fails: The Texas Floods

What if we don't get a reliable warning that the disaster is coming? What if there's no one to answer the phone when we call for help? What if some of the damage could have been avoided?

On the night of July 4, 2025, historic flash flooding tore through Kerr County, Texas. More than 130 people were killed, including children swept away from their summer camp cabins. Entire neighborhoods were destroyed.

In the aftermath, multiple failures became clear:

- The local National Weather Service office had no warning coordination manager after the position was eliminated during staffing cuts.

- Hundreds of FEMA call-center contractors were laid off *during the emergency*, leaving tens of thousands of calls unanswered.
- Federal disaster-preparedness funds that had been allocated to the region were never spent by state and local officials.
- Statewide, Texas had declined or returned hundreds of millions of dollars meant for flood mitigation and resilient infrastructure.

No single failure caused the disaster. But together, they meant that the community was not prepared for such a disaster, warnings came later, help arrived slower, and recovery became harder and more chaotic.

What if fire season comes, and we aren't ready?

How many people are really needed in firefighting? I thought most fire departments were staffed with volunteers? What do firefighters do when there's no fire?

Wildfires are no longer rare events. Nearly 9 million acres burned in the U.S. in 2024 alone. According to FEMA, almost the entire western half of the country is at high risk of wildfire. And, as we saw during the LA fires that destroyed thousands of structures, drove people from their homes, and forced the evacuation of entire cities, all it takes is a strong wind to bring a fire that started in the "wild" into an urban center. This is why prevention, not just response, is a key element of fire safety. Fire prevention depends on lots of people doing unglamorous work long before flames appear—clearing brush, managing forests, training crews, upgrading equipment. When that work is cut, the consequences are measured in lives, homes, and entire communities erased.

Right now, there are big changes afoot in the National Forest Service and other agencies whose work is related to preventing wildfires. Training at the National Fire Academy was paused without explanation for several months in 2025. The National Forest Service lost thousands of employees. And funding and staff cuts that were in place at the National Institute for Occupational Safety and Health for almost nine months put critical firemen's health research and protections at risk.

Firefighters, and the nation, are being promised a more efficient and effective fire prevention and firefighting service in the newly formed "U.S. Wildland Fire Service". But, cuts to various agencies that contribute to fire prevention and fighting - the National Park Service, the National Forest Service, the Bureau of Land Management - are making some experts worry that the new agency may lack resources and expertise. Meanwhile, cuts in FEMA grants could leave communities and agencies with fewer resources for prevention and remediation.

What if the National Guard is busy somewhere else?

I thought the National Guard was for military use, what else do they do to protect our security? Does the National Guard have expertise that is useful for keeping the peace at home? What kinds of domestic emergencies does the National Guard respond to?

The National Guard is more than just a combat reserve. National Guardsmen are also often the backbone of disaster response to domestic disasters ranging from destructive severe weather events to epidemics of disease. FEMA and the National Guard work together to coordinate the movement of supplies and equipment, as well as search and rescue operations, and supply water and food in the wake of natural disasters. In 2022 alone, nearly 200,000 Guard members - that's almost half of all National Guardsmen - worked in disaster recovery and emergency response across the country. When they're deployed for natural disasters, the federal government covers the cost.

These services of the National Guard are very important to our safety and security. But the Guard is now being pulled in new directions and used for different purposes. In 2025, thousands of Guard members were federalized and deployed for immigration enforcement and domestic law enforcement operations unrelated to disaster response. Proposals to expand this role—and talk of invoking the Insurrection Act—raise serious concerns about whether Guard units will be available to help when hurricanes, floods, or fires strike.

Security isn't just about having troops. It's about having them in the right place, at the right time, doing the right job. When disaster response competes with political priorities, everyone is less safe.

What if the nonprofits holding communities together collapse?

What if community safety programs disappear? Why do we spend money on programs that deal with things that haven't happened yet - How does that make us safer?

Public safety isn't only about emergency response. It's also about prevention. In an ideal world, the emergencies would never happen. In this world, federal grants to state, local, and national public safety nonprofits support prevention programs designed to remove people from dangerous situations, treat addictions and illnesses that can lead to violence, and foster trust between community members and law enforcement so people feel safe reporting a danger before it becomes an emergency. These nonprofits provide hundreds of services, including:

- Community policing
- Violence interruption programs
- Domestic violence prevention
- Mental health and addiction treatment
- Re-entry programs that reduce repeat offenses

Cuts to these programs don't make communities safer. They push problems downstream—into emergency rooms, jails, and court systems that are already stretched thin. Federal law enforcement agencies have also severed ties with civil-rights and extremism watchdog organizations that help identify threats before violence occurs.

Many public safety services are delivered by nonprofits: shelters, hotlines, addiction treatment centers, youth programs, and violence-prevention groups. And most of them rely on federal grants to fund at least part of their difficult, unglamorous but very important work. In fact, federal grants make up about one-third of nonprofit revenue nationwide. And tens of thousands of organizations rely on them for more than half their funding. When those grants are frozen, cut, or denied for political reasons, these organizations don't "scale back." They shut down. And when they do, communities lose not just services—but jobs, stability, and trust.

Bottom Line

Security isn't just police or soldiers. It's preparation, prevention, coordination, and trust. It's:

- The warning that comes in time
- The firefighter who's trained and equipped
- The Guard unit that's available when disaster strikes
- The shelter that stays open
- The phone that gets answered

When public safety systems are cut, redirected, or politicized, the damage doesn't always show up right away. But when the moment comes—and it always does—you find out what's missing.

CHAPTER 7
YOUR WORK: PAYCHECKS AND PAPERWORK

SBA LOANS, OSHA, LABOR LAWS, NLRB, EEOC, DOL, EBSA, UNEMPLOYMENT INSURANCE, JOB CORPS

Work is how most people access the economy. It's where you spend your time and expend your energy in exchange for the compensation that you need to support yourself and your family. It's the paycheck that arrives—or doesn't. The schedule you're given—or can't change. The benefits you rely on—or lose. The safety rules that protect you—or quietly disappear.

We're taught to think of jobs as a private relationship between a worker and an employer who, ostensibly, set their own terms. But the truth is, unless you're the only person around who can do your job, employers have a lot more power to set the terms of employment than workers do. That's why a lot of the employer-worker relationship is shaped by public rules designed to protect workers: what the minimum wage is, how many hours you can - or can be required to - work, whether your job is safe, whether you can organize with coworkers, and what happens if you get hurt, sick, laid off, or decide to start something of your own.

When those rules are enforced, work is more predictable and fair—even when it's hard.

When they aren't, the balance of power between employers and workers shifts fast. And workers feel it immediately.

What if my job suddenly became more dangerous?

Are there health hazards in my workplace? Will I even know? Will I be given protective equipment? Will I get healthcare if I'm injured or become sick because of toxins or dangerous materials at my job? What if I see something dangerous at my job, will I get fired if I complain about it? How many people have been hurt or become sick doing this job? Can my employer force me to work in the sun all day without breaks or water?

Many people assume that if something is unsafe at work, someone is watching and trying to minimize the danger. That assumption exists because of laws passed decades ago—and the agencies that enforce them. The Occupational Safety and Health Administration (OSHA) sets and enforces safety standards that apply to every kind of work environment. If you work in construction, manufacturing, extraction, agriculture, forestry, shipping, firefighting, retail sales, or even just in an office, OSHA rules protect you.

OSHA inspects workplaces, investigates workplace injuries and deaths, and protects workers who speak up about dangerous conditions. Its scientific arm, the National Institute for Occupational Safety and Health (NIOSH), researches workplace hazards—everything from loose electrical wiring to toxic chemicals and heat exposure—and provides the evidence that underpins safety rules.

Together, these agencies make sure that:

- Employers provide protective equipment
- Employees are educated about dangerous materials and equipment
- Dangerous materials are handled safely
- Workers aren't fired for reporting hazards
- New risks are identified, and safety protocols are put in place before they cause injuries

But those protections depend on OSHA and NIOSH being staffed and doing the work of both rulemaking and inspections.

NIOSH has been virtually inoperable since April of 2025, when 90% of its workforce were sent layoff notices. Though the administration rescinded the layoff notices in January of 2026, the agency is in disarray, has lost nine months of work, and may not be able to retain expert staff in its current unstable environment. OSHA, meanwhile, has seen cuts to both staff and budget, forcing it to reduce inspections and slow rulemaking. Fewer inspectors mean fewer workplace visits. Fewer researchers mean fewer updates to safety standards—even as jobs change and new risks emerge.

What does that mean in real life? It means hazards go unstudied. Complaints go unanswered. Fire evacuation plans go unupdated. Inspections could be delayed until after someone is hurt—or killed.

If you work in firefighting, in coal mining or extraction, in a warehouse, on a construction site, in agriculture, healthcare, or manufacturing, OSHA protections aren't abstract. They determine whether you're given protective equipment, whether there are set water breaks during extreme heat, whether equipment is properly maintained, and whether speaking up about hazards costs you your job.

When enforcement weakens, safety becomes optional—or a cost v. benefit analysis for employers - and workers pay the price with their bodies.

What if I don't get paid what I'm owed?

What if I don't get my overtime pay or the overtime rules change? What if my employer doesn't pay the legal minimum wage? What if my employer withholds pay or doesn't pay for a long time? What if my employer tries to pay with something other than money - like certificates to the company cafeteria? Am I an employee or an independent contractor? How does this impact my rights to pay or benefits? Can an employer pay me less, or refuse to employ me because I am black, gay, female, Latina, or Muslim? What if a family member gets sick? Will I lose my job if I need to take time off to take care of them? Am I an independent contractor even if this is my only job and I've worked onsite, full-time, for years?

Wage theft is one of the most common crimes in the country. It can take many forms: Unpaid overtime. Missed minimum wage. Paychecks that arrive late—or never. Workers misclassified as "independent contractors" to avoid paying benefits.

The Department of Labor enforces wage and hour laws, many of which are laid out in the Fair Labor Standards Act (FLSA), through its Wage and Hour Division. Wage and Hour investigates worker complaints, recovers stolen wages, and enforces rules around overtime, child labor, and family leave. But enforcement can only happen if investigators are encouraged - and allowed - to investigate.

Budget cuts and policy changes are leaving millions of routine violations untouched and inviting employers to self-police. While at the same time, the administration has walked away from defending stronger overtime rules, protecting workers from misclassification as independent contractors, and has eliminated higher minimum wage standards for federal contractors.

The result is predictable:

- More unpaid hours
- Fewer consequences for employers
- Harder choices for workers already living paycheck to paycheck

When you don't have the power to negotiate the terms of your employment individually—which most people don't—The rules (previously) enforced by the Department of Labor are the only thing standing between fair pay and exploitation.

What if I try to organize—and there's no one to protect me?

Can I be fired for joining a union? Can I be fired for asking for a raise? Does my boss or the owner of the company I work for have to listen to the concerns of employees? Am I allowed to join with other workers who have the same concerns as I do and approach the boss together?

For many workers, organizing with coworkers is the only way to achieve fair pay, predictable scheduling, benefits, and safety. The right to organize with coworkers without retaliation from employers exists because of the National Labor Relations Act, which is enforced by the National Labor Relations Board (NLRB).

The NLRB investigates unfair labor practices. It protects workers from retaliation for organizing and ensures employers negotiate in good faith when workers form unions.

But the agency has been weakened deliberately.

The NLRB operated without a quorum for nearly the entirety of 2025, delaying important decisions. Staff positions have been cut. And, its independence is under direct legal and political attack by employers seeking to roll back decades of worker protections.

When enforcement stalls, conflicts between employers and unions intensify, and the message received by unions may be that they are entirely on their own, with no one in government protecting their right to negotiate when working conditions are unsafe or unfair. Uncertainty as to the stability of the NLRB may also chill organizing efforts or embolden employers to attempt to prevent employees from organizing altogether.

Without a functioning referee, power flows one way.

What if my benefits shrink—or disappear?

Does my full-time employer have to provide healthcare benefits? Can my employer give different benefits to different employees? What if I lose my job? How long will my health coverage last? Can my employer-sponsored health insurer deny me coverage if I have a pre-existing condition? Is my pension guaranteed to be there when I retire? What if I have a mental health issue, such as depression or ADHD, will my medication be covered?

For most Americans, healthcare and retirement savings don't come from the government. They come from work. You are presented with your health plan options when you get your job offer. Many people remain in, or take, certain jobs that sponsor the health plans they rely on to keep their families healthy. You allow your HR department to make automatic contributions to your 401K and to determine how that money is managed and invested.

Employer-sponsored health insurance covers more than 140 million people. Employer-sponsored retirement plans hold more than $14 trillion in assets. The rules that protect those benefits are enforced by the Employee Benefits Security Administration (EBSA), which oversees employer-sponsored health plans and retirement accounts under ERISA, the Employee Retirement Income Security Act.

Those rules ensure that:

- Employers clearly explain what plans cover
- Workers can't be denied coverage for pre-existing conditions
- Health plans treat mental health care on par with physical care
- Retirement savings aren't quietly drained by excessive fees or lost to risky investments

But EBSA has lost about 20% of its staff, and enforcement priorities are shifting.

Mental health parity rules have already been weakened for employer-sponsored health care plans, meaning that workers with ADHD or depression may not receive the health care they need. Oversight of retirement plan investments is also being loosened. All while lower staffing at the agency means changes to the enforcement of all rules -- fewer audits, fewer penalties, and more room for abuse.

For workers, that means:

- Higher out-of-pocket health costs
- Mental health care becomes harder to access
- Less transparency about retirement savings
- Greater risk that benefits erode without warning

You may not notice right away. But, next year, or years from now, when you need care, or retire, you'll feel the difference.

What if I lose my job—and there's no safety net?

What if I lose my job? What if my job was the only one I was qualified for? I can't afford college or trade school, how can I learn a skill? What if unemployment skyrockets in my State, will people still have access to unemployment benefits?

Losing a job doesn't just mean losing a paycheck. It means losing stability in many areas of life - paying for rent or groceries or medicines or a tank of gas so you can get to the next job interview.

Unemployment insurance is supposed to help workers through the transition from one job to the next - to help you stay afloat so you *can* get another job. States pay for the unemployment benefits themselves, but the federal government pays for the systems that make those benefits work: the technology, claims processing, and the workforce development programs that help people get new jobs. Cuts to the Department of Labor threaten that infrastructure, and it is not infrastructure that states can easily or inexpensively recreate on their own.

Workforce development programs, often funded

through federal grants, that help people learn new skills or find new work are being eliminated or consolidated into smaller, less effective programs.

One of the biggest potential losses is the Job Corps—a program that has trained more than 2 million young people over its history. Centers have already been closed or threatened with closure, leaving tens of thousands of low-income young adults without access to the skills training, housing, and job-seeking support that Job Corps provides.

When unemployment rises—and it always does during economic shifts—cuts to the infrastructure of unemployment benefits mean longer waits, fewer opportunities, higher costs for states, and more people slipping into long-term unemployment.

What if I want to start a business—but can't get a loan?

What if I need a loan to get my business off the ground? What if the banks turn me down even though I have a good business plan and just need the capital? What if I have a great business idea, but I need money for space or equipment or employees to get started? What if I offer a service and really just need to paint my truck and get my name out there in my community, but I don't have the money for that? What if I found a great business that I want to buy, but I don't have enough for the downpayment? What if I have a valuable skill, but just don't know how to manage my work as a business?

Small businesses are the backbone of local economies and the meeting place of communities. They are lumber mills and yoga studios, trucking companies and cupcake stands, landscaping firms and interior designers, your local vet's office and the cobbler around the corner, a plumber and an accountant... They are run by people who pursued a dream of building something of their own, *and* they employ more than 60 million people - that's more than 40% of all private sector workers.

For many of these entrepreneurs, the Small Business Administration is foundational to their ability to start and run a business. Not only are SBA-backed loans often the only way to raise the money needed to get the doors open, the SBA also provides the training and coaching needed to run a business. The SBA guarantees loans, provides skills training, and offers ongoing support and advocacy for small businesses through local offices across the country.

More than 30 million small businesses, employing 40% of the workforce and generating more than 40% of US GDP, have or currently rely on the SBA.

But the SBA is facing deep cuts:

- Nearly 43% of its workforce
- A third of its budget

- The elimination of programs like SCORE, Women's Business Centers, and Veterans Business Outreach

At the same time, SBA funding is being politicized —threatened or withdrawn from cities based on unrelated immigration policies.

For someone trying to run, start, or buy a business, that means:

- Fewer loans approved
- Less guidance navigating permits, payroll, and taxes
- Entire communities losing access to capital

This moment in history, when automation and AI are reshaping white-collar work, and when millions of baby boomer–owned businesses are up for sale, is exactly the wrong time to weaken government support for entrepreneurship.

Bottom Line

Your job isn't just about effort or attitude. It's shaped by:

- Safety rules that keep you alive
- Wage laws that ensure you're paid what you're owed

- Benefit protections that guard your health and retirement
- Unemployment systems that catch you when you fall and help you get on your feet again
- Small business programs that create opportunity

When those systems are cut, weakened, or politicized, work becomes riskier, less stable, and less fair—especially for people with the least power to absorb the shock.

If the inspection doesn't happen…

If the overtime rule isn't enforced…

If the benefits suddenly change...

If bridge loans are not available...

If job-training programs shut down...

If you lose your job for reporting a hazard...

CHAPTER 8
YOUR HOBBIES: PLAYGROUNDS, PARKS, AND PUBLIC POOLS

NATIONAL PARK SERVICE, NATIONAL ENDOWMENTS FOR THE ARTS AND HUMANITIES, INSTITUTE OF MUSEUM AND LIBRARY SERVICES, THE LAND AND WATER CONSERVATION FUND

For most people, hobbies are where life happens outside of work. They're where kids burn off energy after school. Where families gather on weekends. Where seniors walk, read, and meet friends. Where towns celebrate, grieve, and come together.

A playground.

A park bench.

A library card.

A free concert.

A public pool on a hot day.

These things feel ordinary. They feel local. They feel like they belong to the community. But almost all of them exist with at least some federal financial support. And when that support is cut, the losses are immediate and personal. Not symbolic. Not abstract. Just gone.

What if my local park closed?

What if the project to build the ballpark was abandoned halfway through? What if National Parks don't open this summer? Where will we go hiking? What if our park is turned into a quarry? What if the Fish and Wildlife Service takes forever to issue permits this year?

What's better than a day at the park? Sure, that's different for everyone... Some of us go to watch birds, others to play baseball. You might take a brisk walk, someone else might cast a fishing line into a lake while their family sets up a picnic. But however you most enjoy them, parks are shared spaces that people across the country treasure.

We are lucky to have a large number and variety of parks in our country. But maintaining them is a big public investment. Public parks across the country are bought and maintained through a mix of local budgets and federal funds. Federal funds play a big role in land acquisition, maintenance, and improvements for parks.

Where does the money for all these parks come from?

Much of the federal financial support for parks comes from the Land and Water Conservation Fund (LWCF). The money in the fund doesn't come from tax dollars.

It comes from royalties that private companies pay the government in return for using public lands. It's a pretty simple concept: when private companies extract oil, gas, or minerals from public land, they pay royalties to the federal government. A small share of the royalties is set aside to preserve land and build parks. You're not paying for the park; a company that dug one park is paying for the purchase and maintenance of other parks.

LWCF funds have helped build or improve more than 40,000 parks and recreation projects across the country—everything from ballfields and boat ramps to urban playgrounds and walking trails. They generate real public benefits - access to green spaces and waterways, and the creation of spaces that communities treasure.

The LWCF was supposed to be permanently funded with $900 million per year through the Great American Outdoors Act of 2020. But now, the Administration and the Department of the Interior are seeking to divert more than $200 million to the "deferred maintenance program", essentially arguing that we do not need to purchase more public lands. Instead of increasing our investment in parks, there have been proposals to sell public lands and also an increase in permits for extraction on public lands.

Meanwhile, grants for urban parks and underserved communities have already been paused. And deeper cuts to the National Park Service—up to 30% of its budget—threaten closures, reduced hours, and fewer rangers on the ground.

For communities near national parks, these cuts aren't just about scenery. National parks support over 400,000 jobs and generate tens of billions of dollars in local economic activity. When parks close or degrade, entire towns feel it—hotels, restaurants, outfitters, guides, scientists, and seasonal workers.

And in cities, when a local park loses funding, it doesn't "decline gracefully." Bathrooms close. Playgrounds break. Fields go unmaintained. Safety declines.

What if public land just wasn't public anymore?

For generations, public land has served many purposes at once: conservation, recreation, education, limited extraction, and long-term stewardship. That balance is shifting.

While proposals to directly sell off millions of acres of public lands failed to pass Congress as part of the One Big Beautiful Bill Act, the Department of the Interior (DOI) has taken actions to reduce protections and increase exploitation on public lands. These include the elimination of the roadless rule that protected our national forests, the rolling back or non-enforcement of environmental and endangered species protections that prevented destructive exploitation in fragile areas like the Arctic, and prohibitions of extractive activities in midwestern boundary waters. These rule reversals and non-enforcement actions will open up more than 100 million acres of public land to exploitation and remove them from conservation and public use.

Public land isn't just open space. It's a shared inheritance. Selling it or opening vast amounts of it to exploitation by private companies leaves communities poorer - financially and culturally.

What if community gathering places disappear?

Will there be Shakespeare in the park this summer? My kid really likes classical music, could she go to a concert in town? I want to learn about the people who lived in this land before our town was incorporated. Can the town set up an exhibit about it? We want to bring this amazing performance troupe to our town's summer festival, how can we afford it?

Libraries and arts programs are so important and enriching for communities. They create children's first experiences with art and live music. They give adults the opportunity to learn new skills or find out things they never knew about local history. Concerts and theater performances are events that communities look forward to all year long. Field trips to local museums and libraries open kids' eyes to so many things to create and learn and think about.

But, of course, these wonderful services aren't free. They rely on federal, state, local, and private funds to keep running. The federal government supports local libraries, the arts and humanities through three small federal agencies:

- The National Endowment for the Arts
- The National Endowment for the Humanities
- The Institute of Museum and Library Services

Together, their budgets are tiny compared to most federal programs. But their impact is enormous. They fund:

- Museum exhibits and school trips
- Free concerts, theater, and festivals
- Library staffing and training
- Story time and early literacy programs
- Adult education, GED prep, and digital skills
- Access to computers, printers, and the internet

When these agencies are cut or eliminated entirely, local institutions don't have a backup plan. Small towns can't replace federal arts funding. Libraries can't absorb sudden budget holes. Museums can't keep programs running on ticket sales alone. When grants disappear, programs shut down. Staff are laid off. Doors close. And the loss is felt most by families who can't afford private lessons, summer camps, or enrichment programs.

What if my local library wasn't there?

Where can mom learn to use a computer or how to claim her social security? Where can we take the kids on a rainy day? I like books by a certain author, where can I find more of them other than at the store? We want to have a meeting with our group of local history buffs, where can we do that?

The public library is a central feature of many communities. It's where kids learn to love reading. Where seniors learn to use email. Where people apply for jobs, benefits, and healthcare. Where students study and where grown-ups slip away to read quietly. Libraries host community events - story time for children, guest speakers about topics of interest to the community. They house works of art and culture that enrich all of our lives - books, movies, microfilm... And, they are dedicated spaces open to all members of the community; sometimes a blessedly cool place where someone without air conditioning can spend a hot afternoon.

The money for libraries comes from a mix of local, state, and federal funds. Federal Funds for libraries come from the Institute of Museum and Library Services, which is the largest source of federal funding for public libraries. Its grants support not just buildings, but inter-library lending, digitization, workforce training, and statewide library systems. Some towns might be able to afford to keep their libraries open without this funding. But others would see a sharp decrease in what their local library could offer or even how many days a week it would be open. In early 2025, the administration issued an executive order eliminate IMLS and later requested a budget calling for only the funds needed to wind down the program. It wasn't until December of 2025 that IMLS grants were restored. When IMLS staff were put on leave and funding was frozen, libraries across the country immediately felt the impact—uncertainty about staffing, canceled programs, and delayed upgrades.

Libraries don't disappear overnight. But they hollow out. Hours get cut. Programs vanish. Services narrow.

And once they're gone, they're hard to rebuild.

What if art and culture became a luxury?

Arts and humanities funding is often dismissed as "nice to have." But for many communities, it's how people come together: A summer concert in the park. A local theater production. A history exhibit that tells a town's story. A poetry program in a town whose school doesn't have one.

And, federal arts and humanities grants don't just fund art. They also legitimize it. Winning a grant helps organizations raise additional money from private donors and foundations. When those grants are canceled—as hundreds already have been—entire ecosystems collapse. What remains is a cultural divide: arts thrive in wealthy areas with higher local budgets or private funding, while everyone else loses access.

Art becomes something you buy, rather than something you share.

Bottom Line

Parks, libraries, pools, museums, and arts programs aren't extras. Public infrastructure is foundational to community life.

They're where communities make memories. Where kids grow. Where people come together, learn, and belong.

When these systems are cut, life doesn't just get harder—it gets smaller.

If the park closes…

If the library cuts hours…

If the museum shuts its doors…

If the playground rusts and breaks…

You lose more than a place to go. You lose the shared spaces that make a community feel like home. And once they're gone, they're much harder—and much more expensive—to bring back.

CHAPTER 9
YOUR UTILITIES: LIGHTS ON, BILLS PAID

WATER TREATMENT, ELECTRIC GRID REGULATION, LIHEAP, BROADBAND EXPANSION, CLEAN ENERGY FUNDING

You don't think about utilities—until they stop working, or the bill comes.

You turn on the faucet and assume the water is safe. You flip a switch and expect the lights to come on. In winter, the heat kicks in. In summer, the air conditioner hums. When your child logs into school or you open your laptop for work, the internet connects.

Utilities feel automatic. But they are not automatic. They are the product of constant public investment: pipes replaced before they fail, dams monitored and calibrated, power plants regulated, transmission lines upgraded, broadband laid across miles of rural land, safety standards enforced, and assistance programs helping families keep the lights on.

When those systems weaken, the damage doesn't always make national news. It shows up somewhere smaller and more personal — on your monthly bill, in your drinking water, on your child's laptop, or in your ability to survive a heat wave.

Utilities are invisible right up until they aren't.

What if you weren't sure your water was safe to drink?

Will I be able to tell if there's something bad in the water? What if the pipe-replacement project stalls halfway through? Were all of those new rules about water contaminants just overkill? Our town water seems to work just fine. Why mess with it?

You turn on the tap. It looks clear. It smells fine. But you can't see lead. You can't taste PFAS — the so-called "forever chemicals" linked to cancer and other serious health conditions. You can't detect most contaminants without testing and enforcement.

More than 200 million Americans are exposed to potential drinking water contamination risks. As recently as 2023, roughly 9 percent of U.S. water lines were still lead pipes — remnants of infrastructure laid generations ago and never fully replaced.

After the Flint water crisis, Congress approved billions of dollars to replace those pipes nationwide. That investment was meant to fix a problem we already knew existed. Now those funds are facing reductions. Proposed budgets scale back the state revolving funds that cities rely on to repair and modernize drinking water systems, shifting more of the burden onto states, municipalities, and ultimately ratepayers.

At the same time, enforcement of clean water standards has slowed. Rules governing PFAS contamination have been weakened or postponed. Monitoring requirements are under review.

Water systems rarely collapse overnight. They deteriorate gradually. Maintenance is deferred. Testing becomes less frequent. Replacement projects are delayed. And then, one day, contamination is discovered — and the cost of fixing it falls squarely on families and local communities.

The danger isn't always dramatic. It's cumulative.

What if I live in the West—and someone else controls my water?

Will the water used for the farms mean there's less drinking water for our city? Why can't I just water my lawn whenever I want? I live in L.A., why do Colorado and Wyoming get to tell us how much water we can use?

If you live in the West, water carries another layer of risk. In western states, water is stored and routed through vast systems of dams and reservoirs managed by the Bureau of Reclamation and the U.S. Army Corps of Engineers. Farmers depend on these systems for irrigation. Cities depend on them for drinking supply. Hydropower facilities depend on them to generate electricity.

For example, forty million people depend on the Colorado river for fresh water supply. It affects people in many states. Those to the north, where the water "comes from", and those to the south that are much dryer, but have much larger populations. In 2026, following an extremely dry winter that has led to much lower water levels in the Colorado river, the States reliant on the watershed area, must reach an agreement that will require painful sacrifices both in the north and the south. This touches all people and industry in the area. How much and when can farmers water crops? Are the water levels sufficient to power the hydro-dams that provide electricity? How about individuals? Not just watering lawns, but also drinking, bathing, cooking...Who would be prioritized if States fail to reach an agreement and the Department of the Interior sets the rules? Would cities like Phoenix have enough fresh water to support their populations?

Managing that balance requires staffing, engineering expertise, and stable funding. Recent budget proposals would cut hundreds of millions of dollars from the Bureau of Reclamation and reduce staffing significantly. At the same time, direct political intervention in dam operations has introduced instability — including sudden water releases that flooded downstream communities and deprived farms of irrigation water needed for future growing seasons.

Water management is not an ideology. It is math and physics. Flood control must be balanced against irrigation. Drinking water must be balanced against power generation. When that balance is disrupted, farmers lose crops, electricity production drops, and food prices rise. What appears to be a policy decision in Washington becomes a grocery bill in your kitchen.

What if my power bill keeps going up—and I don't know why?

Why is power getting more expensive even though there are so many empty office buildings? I thought we were generating more energy, where's it all going? We're trying to use less heat and AC to save on electric bills, is there anything else we can do?

Over the past several years, electricity prices have risen dramatically in states across the country. There are a lot of reasons - increased demand, aging infrastructure, fuel prices...To name a few. Millions of Americans are either behind on their energy bills, or need financial assistance to afford them. Millions more are nervous - and angry - when their energy bill arrives each month.

At the same time, electricity demand is rising rapidly, even in places where populations are stable or shrinking. The modern economy runs on power. Data centers alone — more than 5,000 of them across the United States — consume enormous amounts of electricity. A single large data center can use as much power in a month as multiple homes use in a year. The Department of Energy estimates data centers already account for roughly 4 percent of total U.S. electricity consumption, and that share could triple within a few years.

Meeting that demand requires expanding supply and modernizing the grid. That is where federal clean energy investments — in solar, wind, battery storage, and transmission upgrades — have played a role. Proposed rollbacks would eliminate billions of dollars in Department of Energy funding, phase out tax credits for residential solar and electric vehicles, and cancel support for national EV charging infrastructure.

When supply tightens while demand grows, utilities pass the cost on to consumers. Analysts estimate that repealing these investments could increase average household electricity bills by $100 to $160 per year by 2030 — and significantly more beyond that.

Now imagine not being able to pay it.

What if I can't afford to keep the heat or AC on?

Extreme heat and cold are deadly. For decades, the Low Income Home Energy Assistance Program — LIHEAP — has helped millions of Americans afford their heating and cooling bills. While LIHEAP was ultimately funded for 2026, the President's Budget request initially proposed eliminating the program entirely. Meanwhile, changes to SNAP will reduce the ability of families to deduct utility expenses when calculating their eligibility for food assistance and internet access will no longer qualify as a utility expense in those calculations. People already struggling will face even more difficult choices - a bag of beans is a healthy and affordable food option, but they have to be boiled for hours before you can eat them, which takes energy, which costs me money.

When energy bills rise and assistance disappears, families don't magically find new income. They turn down the thermostat. They skip air conditioning during heat waves. They fall behind on payments. Shutoffs follow.

Utility insecurity becomes housing insecurity very quickly.

What if my child's school closes—and I don't have the internet?

The pandemic made something clear: broadband is essential infrastructure. Students attend school online. Adults work remotely. Job applications are digital. Medical appointments happen over video. Today, more than 90 percent of jobs require some level of digital skill.

Yet roughly 24 million Americans still lack reliable high-speed broadband.

The Broadband Equity, Access, and Deployment (BEAD) program was designed to close that gap with more than $40 billion in funding. That funding is now being reshaped and conditioned on unrelated political provisions, slowing deployment even where money technically remains available.

Without reliable broadband, students fall behind. Workers lose opportunities. Small businesses struggle to compete. Telehealth disappears. The digital divide isn't merely inconvenient; it locks communities out of economic growth.

What if my job depends on the energy transition?

What were all those manufacturing jobs that disappeared this year? What happened to that solar plant they were building outside of town? My kid is studying to be an electrical engineer, is that still a good choice?

An energy transition wouldn't just lower emissions, it would create jobs. Since 2022, federal clean energy investments have driven more than $200 billion in private investment and supported the creation of hundreds of thousands of jobs — many in rural and conservative districts. Battery manufacturing plants, solar factories, EV assembly lines, and wind farm construction projects have reshaped local economies. But, rolling back tax credits and canceling grant programs has paused construction. It froze hiring. It has deterred private capital. And, the jobs at stake are often skilled manufacturing and construction positions that anchor small towns.

Energy policy determines where factories are built — and whether they are built at all.

Bottom Line

Clean water.

Reliable electricity.

Affordable heat and air conditioning.

Internet access.

These are not luxuries. They are the baseline conditions of modern life.

Utilities form the foundation beneath everything else.

If water systems fail, property values decline.

If electricity costs rise, inflation rises.

If broadband access is uneven, opportunity becomes uneven.

If energy assistance disappears, homelessness increases.

Utilities are not partisan. They are structural.

When they weaken, communities weaken. When funding is cut, enforcement delayed, or infrastructure politicized, the costs do not disappear. They shift. From shared public investment to individual households.

Bills rise.

Risks rise.

Security shrinks.

If the pipes aren't replaced, if the grid isn't modernized, if assistance vanishes — you don't simply lose convenience. You lose stability.

CHAPTER 10

YOUR FAMILY: IN SICKNESS AND IN HEALTH INSURANCE

HEADSTART, MATERNITY CARE, CHILDCARE SUBSIDIES, THE FMLA

In the Healthcare chapter, we talked about what happens when hospitals close, when research slows, when Medicaid shrinks.

But healthcare doesn't begin in an emergency room.

It begins much earlier — when you decide to have a child. When you bring that child home. When you try to balance work, childcare, and bills. When you need time to recover. When you need time to care.

Family policy isn't separate from healthcare policy.

It is healthcare policy — stretched across time.

What if I find out I'm pregnant — and don't know how I'll pay for care?

We want to have a baby, but how can we afford it? I have private insurance, but I live in a rural area, will cuts to medicaid affect my local healthcare services? What if I or my baby get sick after my baby is born, how will I get care?

Having a baby is a big decision for anyone. You worry about how you'll afford books and toys and birthday parties and schools and trips to amazing places for your kids. But, all of that comes after the cost of being pregnant and safely giving birth to your baby. The average cost of giving birth in the United States is nearly $19,000.That figure doesn't include months of prenatal visits, possible complications, or extended postpartum care. For many families, that cost alone would be destabilizing.

More than 41 percent of births in America are covered by Medicaid. That statistic doesn't just reflect families in deep poverty. It includes working families with part-time jobs, rural families without employer coverage, and women whose employer plans do not fully cover maternity care.

When Medicaid funding is cut, the consequences ripple outward to all kinds of healthcare. When hospitals lose reliable reimbursement, departments close. Services shrink. And maternity wards are often among the first to go.

What if my nearest maternity ward closed?

Since 2022, more than 100 maternity units have closed across the country. Today, millions of women live in what are known as "maternity care deserts" — counties without obstetric services, birthing centers, or hospital delivery units.

Even if you have private insurance, if your local maternity ward shuts down, you still have to drive farther to deliver a baby. You still face longer wait times. You still rely on the same strained healthcare system.

When Medicaid shrinks, pregnancy becomes riskier for everyone.

The United States already has the highest maternal mortality rate among high-income countries. Reducing Medicaid funding won't just affect "other people." It will destabilize healthcare, and maternity care, in entire regions.

The Big Beautiful Bill Act will cut hundreds of billions of dollars from Medicaid over the next decade. It will eliminate or reduce the enhanced federal match for Medicaid expansion states. They will limit how states use provider taxes to finance their Medicaid systems. And, the new work requirements will remove millions of people from coverage.

Lawmakers often note that pregnant women are exempt from some of these work requirements. But hospitals do not operate maternity wards in isolation. Clinics do not exist separately from the broader patient base.

When millions of adults lose coverage, hospital

revenue declines. When revenue declines, departments close. Rural hospitals, already operating on thin margins, shutter entirely.

You cannot cut the financing of the system and expect the services to remain untouched.

Up to 20 million people could lose coverage over the next decade. When that many patients disappear from the insurance rolls, hospitals cannot simply "adjust." They consolidate. They eliminate services. They close wings.

And when maternity wards close, every pregnancy in that region becomes more dangerous.

What if complications show up weeks later?

Pregnancy does not end at delivery. The postpartum period can bring hemorrhage, infection, blood pressure crises, and severe depression. Many maternal deaths occur weeks after childbirth, not during it.

Medicaid expansion in many states has extended postpartum coverage beyond the traditional cutoff, recognizing that care does not end when a baby leaves the hospital. Proposed cuts — particularly eliminating the enhanced federal match for expansion states — would push millions off coverage once again.

Even narrow policy changes destabilize the whole system. When hospitals close. When clinics reduce staff. When doctors leave rural areas. Access narrows for everyone.

Family policy and hospital policy are not separate conversations. They are the same system viewed from different moments in time.

What if I can't afford childcare — and can't afford not to work?

Childcare in America now averages more than $13,000 per year. In many states, it costs more than rent. For single parents, it can consume a third or more of annual income. Federal programs like Head Start and childcare block grants have helped fill the gap for decades. But funding freezes, regional office closures, and proposed eliminations have destabilized those supports. At the same time, Temporary Assistance for Needy Families — a major source of childcare funding — faces tighter work requirements and reduced flexibility.

This creates an impossible contradiction. Parents have to work to keep a roof over their children's heads. But they cannot afford childcare.

When childcare funding shrinks, parents leave the workforce. Employers struggle to hire. Household income drops. Children lose early learning support that shapes long-term outcomes.

Childcare workers themselves — among the

lowest-paid workers in the economy — often rely on Medicaid, SNAP, or housing assistance. When funding shrinks in one area, pressure builds in others.

It is not a collection of separate programs.

It is one ecosystem.

What if I need time to care for a newborn—or a sick parent?

I've been at my job for years, can my boss just replace me if I get sick and need to be out for a while? My mother suffered a fall and needs me to stay with her for a few weeks while she recovers, but I can't afford to lose my paycheck, what can I do? My husband was injured at his job and needs me to help him get around- how can we make ends meet if we're both out of work for a few days?

The Family and Medical Leave Act guarantees *unpaid,* job-protected leave for certain workers, but only about a quarter of private-sector workers have access to *paid* family leave. Thirteen states have built paid leave systems of their own funded through payroll contributions. But, despite a lot of talk, at the federal level, proposals to expand paid have been stalled for years.

Instead, lawmakers have expanded a voluntary tax credit meant to encourage employers to offer paid leave. That credit has primarily benefited large, profitable companies and has failed to inspire meaningful expansion of access to paid family leave. Meanwhile, policies that make it easier to classify workers as independent contractors have reduced access to leave protections altogether. Gig workers, part-time workers, and many low-income employees often fall outside coverage.

The right to take time off may exist on paper. And maybe you won't get fired for it. But in reality, many families cannot afford to use it.

When parents return to work days after childbirth, medical follow-ups are missed. Recovery is rushed. Care for elderly relatives falls to whoever can absorb the unpaid time. Stress compounds. Health deteriorates quietly.

Time is healthcare, too.

What if the tax credit never arrives?

The Child Tax Credit and the Earned Income Tax Credit are among the most effective anti-poverty programs in the country. When fully refundable and accessible, they reduce child poverty dramatically. But, proposed changes to the Child Tax Credit would leave some of the lowest-income families without access because eligibility is tied to tax liability. You have to owe taxes before you can qualify for the credit, and when the credit is increased, the amount that you have to owe before you can qualify also increases. Meanwhile, new administrative hurdles for the Earned

Income Tax Credit would make it harder for eligible families to receive benefits.

This is a pattern that appears again and again. The program still exists, but it becomes harder to access the benefits. And, the harder it gets the more people not only miss out on one benefit, but experience hardship in even more parts of their lives. When the tax credits fail to reach families, food insecurity rises. Healthcare visits are delayed. Child development suffers. And the effects compound across everything we have already discussed — from hospitals to utilities to schools.

Bottom Line

If you want families to thrive, you need:

Stable maternity care.

Reliable postpartum coverage.

Affordable childcare.

Paid leave that families can actually afford to take.

Tax credits that reach children who need them most.

When those systems are weakened — through funding cuts, staffing losses, administrative barriers, or unstable financing — families absorb the shock first.

But they do not absorb it alone.

If maternity wards close…

If childcare disappears…

If leave is unpaid…

If coverage ends…

Healthcare costs rise.

Workforce participation falls.

Child poverty increases.

You cannot weaken the healthcare system and expect families to remain strong.

CHAPTER 11

YOUR MONEY: DOLLARS AND SENSE

FDIC INSURANCE, SEC REGULATION, RETIREMENT ACCOUNTS, SOCIAL SECURITY

You don't have to think of yourself as "an investor" to be part of the financial system.

If you're paid by direct deposit, you're in it.

If you use a debit card, you're in it.

If you have a 401(k), an IRA, a pension, or a union retirement plan, you're in it.

If you expect to receive Social Security someday, you're in it.

Your money is always somewhere. In a bank. In the markets. In a pension fund. In the Social Security trust fund.

You assume it's safe. You assume it's protected. You assume someone is watching.

Most of the time, those assumptions are correct.

But they are correct because there are rules. And because people enforce those rules.

When rules weaken — or enforcement fades — your money does not just sit there quietly. It becomes more exposed.

What if I woke up and couldn't get my money?

Is my money safe in the bank? What does the bank do with my money? What if I need more money than usual, will I be able to withdraw all of my savings? What if something does happen to my bank? Will I get my money back?

Nearly all American workers are paid by direct deposit. Your paycheck doesn't arrive in cash; it moves electronically into a bank or credit union. But, your money doesn't really go to the bank and sit in a vault labeled with your name. Banks use the money to make loans and investments. That is how they generate profit. In return, they promise that you will be able to access your money when you need it. This system works because, most of the time, not everyone asks for their money at once.

In 2023, Silicon Valley Bank collapsed in a single day after depositors tried to withdraw $42 billion at once. That is what a bank run looks like. When confidence in the bank disappears, everyone tries to get their money at once. And, since the bank has deployed the money in loans and investments, it does not usually have enough cash on hand to pay all of the depositors all of their money all at the same time.

The reason most Americans do not lose all of their savings in moments like that is the Federal Deposit Insurance Corporation — the FDIC. It insures deposits up to $250,000, monitors banks for risky behavior - including their levels of reserve cash kept on hand - and steps in when institutions fail. No insured depositor has ever permanently lost money in an FDIC-insured bank failure. But, the stability that the FDIC provides depends on oversight. It depends on examiners reviewing balance sheets, identifying risky lending, and intervening early.

The FDIC now faces significant staffing cuts — roughly 20 percent of its workforce. At the same time, the Consumer Financial Protection Bureau, created after the 2008 financial crisis to guard against deceptive banking practices, has faced attempts to defund it, severe staffing reductions, and the dismissal of enforcement cases.

When oversight shrinks, risk does not vanish. It builds quietly. Unsafe lending goes unchecked. Consumer complaints sit unresolved.

You don't feel it — until something breaks.

What if my dollar doesn't go as far?

Why is everything getting more expensive? What happened to all of the choices we used to have for products? What if generics were no longer available?

You notice high prices everywhere you look. At the

grocery store. At the hardware store. Online. They're high for a number of reasons. Many products, like food, hardware, clothing, electronics, are imported and travel many miles to get to the shelves of your local store. So, their prices are impacted by how much it costs to get them to you. Tariffs cause their prices to rise. Fuel costs cause their prices to rise. Conflicts that disrupt trade routes cause their prices to rise. Other products are unique or indispensable to the functioning of another product, like the software you use for your job, or the charger that only fits one kind of phone, or the website that you buy concert tickets from. When a product is unique or necessary or if only one company has 80% of the concert tickets to sell, the seller of that product can set a high price regardless of how much it actually costs to make a product.

By now, you're heard about tariffs raising prices. Tariffs raise prices because they are taxes paid by importers. The importer pays more for the things they're importing, and those costs are passed on to customers. This has been big news for months now, with the Supreme Court having recently ruled many of the tariffs set in 2025 and 2026 illegal and speculation now brewing about whether refunds of tariff revenues are due and to whom. But, tariffs are only part of the story of rising prices...

Competition between businesses is what keeps prices down. Producers all vie to make a better product, at a better price and with better customer service to boot, because, in a competitive market customers chose the best product at the best price. In a non-competive market, where monopolies control whole industries, companies can afford to do the bare minimum in terms of quality and service because a monopoly doesn't have to worry about the customer being able go elsewhere with his money.

American antitrust laws exist to prevent monopolies, to stop companies from colluding to set prices or restrict entry of new competitors, and to make sure consumers have real choices.This saves you money, gets you better stuff, *and* supports an economy where there is opportunity and motivation to innovate.

The Department of Justice enforces antitrust laws. When enforcement is strong, companies compete. You can choose between brands. Generic products exist. Prices reflect rivalry rather than dominance. But when enforcement weakens, markets consolidate. Fewer companies control more of the supply chain. Competition shrinks. Prices rise — sometimes gradually, sometimes dramatically. And, quality declines.

The recent budget proposals, and recent action/inaction at the DOJ reflect changing priorities of the anti-trust division. Several mergers of companies that already have massive market share, especially in the digital and entertainment spaces, have been approved. Investigations of proposed mergers are at record lows.

And, officials have signaled a shift away from proactive oversight toward case-by-case litigation after harm has occurred.

The means *after* quality has declined and consumers have paid too much and competitors have been driven from the market. And, once markets consolidate, reversing that consolidation becomes difficult. Intervention arrives late — after smaller competitors have disappeared and consumers are locked in.

When competition weakens, your dollar weakens with it.

What if my retirement savings drop overnight?

I just checked the box that my HR manager suggested for the management of my pension. Is my money safe? Who is overseeing the investment of our pension funds? What if something happens in the markets, will my 401K be safe?

Even if you never trade a stock, your financial security is likely tied to the stock market because retirement accounts — 401(k)s, IRAs, union pensions — invest in public companies to grow. Those markets rise and fall. Some shifts are normal. And, careful decision making can enable investors to earn steady returns on investments.

But, what makes markets work - what makes investment less risky - is transparency. Publicly traded companies have to regularly disclose their financial, and management, information to the public at regular intervals. Company insiders are prohibited from trading stock based on private - inside - information that hasn't been shared with the public. And, fraud is investigated and punished. These safeguards exist because of the Securities and Exchange Commission (SEC).

The SEC was created to restore confidence in financial markets after the crash of 1929 which wiped out the savings of millions of americans. The SEC's job is to require public disclosure, police insider trading, and maintain fair and orderly markets. There has always been push and pull between the SEC and public company executives - compliance with SEC rules is expensive and time consuming, a company may not believe that a quarterly earnings report fairly represents is annual earning potential. But, the transparency that the SEC requires has restored and does help maintain confidence in the financial markets. It is one of the reasons that the savings of so many of us are, more or less confidently, invested in public companies.

Yet today, the SEC faces staff reductions, enforcement slowdowns, and a freeze on new rulemaking. Proposals for cuts to SEC enforcement include reducing disclosure requirements and expanding exemptions that allow companies to sell large amount of stock *without* the same level of public reporting.

Meanwhile, enforcement of laws like the Foreign Corrupt Practices Act - which penalized companies who took illegal or unduly risky actions abroad - has slowed.

All of this makes investment in the stock market riskier. If these companies make fewer disclosures about their business, then investors may not have enough information to make good decisions. When enforcement of the rules slow, instances of fraud increase. This especially impacts ordinary retirement savers who do not have teams of analysts reviewing balance sheets.

Market crashes do not just affect traders on Wall Street. They affect pension funds. They affect workers nearing retirement who suddenly must delay their plans. They affect people who believed they were financially secure — until they weren't.

What if the person managing my pension takes risks I never agreed to?

Is my pension guaranteed no matter what happens to my employer? How do I even know what the person managing my pension is doing? Isn't my employer managing my pension? Are there any protections in place in case my pension is mismanaged?

The Employee Benefits Security Administration (EBSA) oversees roughly $14 trillion in private-sector retirement assets. It enforces "fiduciary" rules that require pension managers to act solely in the best interest of the workers whose money they manage. Your fiduciary is the person or company managing your pension. They not only have to report, both to the department of labor and to you *where* your pension is invested, they also have a duty to invest your pension in the most stable way possible.

EBSA and the fiduciary rules were not created in a vacuum. They were created after pension failures in the 1970s wiped out thousands of workers' savings, prompting Congress to pass ERISA to protect retirement assets. When fiduciary standards are strong, pension managers are accountable. When oversight shrinks, conflicts of interest become harder to detect and riskier investments could be made.

EBSA has already lost a substantial portion of its staff and faces budget reductions. Proposed weakening of fiduciary liability standards will make it harder for workers to challenge misconduct if something goes wrong.

You may never meet the person managing your pension fund. But their decisions can determine whether you retire comfortably — or at all.

What if my Social Security check doesn't arrive on time?

Is my social security guaranteed no matter what happens in the economy or the markets? Will I be able to claim my social security the same way that I always have? Why is there always talk about cutting social security when it's something that we've all paid directly into?

About 67 million Americans rely on Social Security. Nearly 183 million workers contribute to it each year. It is not welfare; it is earned insurance. We pay into the system for decades and expect stability in return. But, demographic changes — especially the retirement of the baby boom generation — mean more people are drawing benefits while fewer workers are contributing. Without congressional action, the social security trust fund could be depleted in the early 2030s.

The Social Security Administration administers this vast, and very popular program. The administration has stated it will not cut benefits. But staffing reductions — roughly 7,000 positions — and tighter identity verification procedures have already created new barriers to access. When field offices close, seniors travel farther for help. When call centers are understaffed, phone lines go unanswered. When paperwork becomes more complicated, delays compound and some people can not manage to make it through the system at all.

And don't forget, Social Security payments not only

support individual retirees. They support local economies — especially in communities with large older populations. Social security payments are spent at pharmacies and stores and markets and on housing and utilities, just the same as regular income. When access to social security payments becomes harder, the harm spreads beyond the individual recipient.

Bottom Line

Financial stability might feel private. How much money you make and how you choose to spend it. It's your paycheck. Your savings. Your retirement account. But the systems protecting that money are public.

When bank oversight weakens, confidence weakens. When antitrust enforcement shrinks, prices rise. When securities enforcement slows, markets grow more volatile. When pension oversight fades, retirement becomes uncertain. When Social Security staffing declines, access narrows.

Each system reinforces the others. If retirees lose savings, they spend less. If banks fail, businesses struggle to make payroll. If markets crash, pensions shrink. If trust erodes, fear spreads quickly.

Your money feels personal. But the safeguards protecting it are structural.

If the FDIC does not monitor banks…

If consumer protection enforcement slows…

If antitrust laws are not enforced…

If the SEC does not require disclosure…

If pension managers are not held to strict fiduciary standards…

If Social Security becomes harder to access…

Risk shifts — from institutions to individuals. And once confidence erodes, it spreads fast.

Your money is only as safe as the rules protecting it. And those rules only work if someone is there to enforce them.

CHAPTER 12
YOUR ENVIRONMENT: THE AIR WE BREATHE AND THE WATER WE DRINK

EPA, CLEAN WATER PROGRAMS, AIR QUALITY STANDARDS

The "environment" isn't just a place you go to study frogs or see exotic birds. It is everywhere that you are, whether you're in an apartment in a big city, on a farm in the great plains, in a suburban office park, or working on an oil rig. Your environment is in the light you see, in the air that you breathe, in the water that you drink, *and also* in the water used to raise the food that you eat. The environment is in the walls of your house, in the halls of your kids' schools, on the road past the factory, in the reservoir, and under the highway overpass.

Sometimes, when something changes in your environment, you sense it right away. You can see and smell the smoke from a wildfire. You get congested if mold starts growing in your home. But other times, maybe even most of the time, you assume everything is fine and that your environment is not harming your health.

You probably don't wake up in the morning and think about environmental law. You breathe. You pour a glass of water. You walk outside. You send your child to school. You assume the air won't make you sick. You assume the water is safe. You assume the land that grows your food isn't poisoned.

And, for a long time, you've been pretty safe in that assumption. Decades of rules, monitoring, enforcement, and scientific research, built in response to disasters many Americans have forgotten, have protected our health and our environment. But we are not all that far away from environmental disasters that wreaked massive costs on health and the environment.

- The Cuyahoga River was so polluted that it caught fire in June of 1969. That was water so polluted that it burned.
- Oil slicks once coated the California coastline. In 1990, one oil tanker spilled 416,000 gallons of crude oil on the California coast.
- Children were poisoned by lead in their drinking water. As recently as 2014, thousands of children were poisoned when their drinking water became contaminated by aged lead pipes.

The modern environmental protection system exists because we've seen what happens when industry operates in and exploits the environment without guardrails. When that system weakens, the damage isn't apparent in headlines about "deregulation" being good for business. It is apparent in:

- Increased cases of asthma.
- Contaminated water.
- Clusters of cancer cases in certain towns.
- Higher medical bills.
- Foul-smelling air.
- Fish that you can catch, but can't eat.
- Strange colored mud flowing into your pond.

And, by the time the source of the damage is identified, it's harder and more expensive to fix.

Why would it matter to me if environmental rules changed?

Do environmental rules just get in the way of progress? Where I live, there's wilderness as far as the eye can see - why shouldn't we get what we can from it? They told us the new plant would bring a lot of jobs - why wouldn't we just let them build it?

You can think about there being two kinds of environmental stewardship. One is "green", and the other is "brown". Green conservation seeks to maintain parts of the environment in as close to their natural state as possible. You see this kind of conservation in national parks. Brown conservation seeks to minimize the harmful effects of necessary industry on our health and on our most important natural resources - water, air, and soil. This kind of conservation involves both the cleanup of polluted sites *and* environmental reviews before new sites can be built. The environmental reviews under the National Environmental Policy Act guide permitting and zoning decisions meant to minimize the environmental impact of new industrial sites.

In other parts of this book, we've talked about cuts to investments in national parks and green spaces, as well as cuts to investment in environmental equity, which sought to improve the environment in some of our most impoverished areas, like inner cities. In this section, we'll talk more about brown conservation.

Right now, environmental reviews are being shortened or bypassed under expedited permitting policies. What this means is that less time is being taken to study what the downstream impacts will be. There are fewer opportunities for the public to provide input. And, there is much less opportunity to prevent long-term damage.

Environmental reviews don't stop development. They slow it down enough to review the costs and the benefits. It asks, is *this* the best place for this development? What will the impact be on the town? On the groundwater? On the air quality? What is the developer's plan to dispose of waste or minimize emissions? What demands will it make on other infrastructure, like water and electrical systems? And, finally, is the trade-off worth it in exchange for the benefits that this development will bring to the community?

When environmental reviews are fast-tracked, minimized, or dispensed with altogether, the risks to communities are real, and the impacts are long-term.

What if it's something in the air?

What if my kids develop asthma? Why are my eyes burning even though it's not allergy season? Why does it seem like everyone has developed a cough? Why is my weather app showing an air quality alert even though it's bright and sunny out? Is this headache really because "the air pressure is changing"?

Air pollution doesn't always look the way it used to. You may not see smog rolling through your city. You might not smell anything unusual. But pollutants from power plants, refineries, cars, trucks, and industrial facilities still enter the air every day.

Since 1970, the Environmental Protection Agency set national air quality standards under the Clean Air Act. Those standards limited how much pollution could be released into the air and were based on evolving scientific knowledge of what levels could be considered safe. The government has funded research into the impact of emissions and air quality for even longer. And, one could argue, a positive result has been that scientists and engineers stepped up to improve the efficiency, not just of cars but of all kinds of machinery that generate emissions. Those improvements lessen environmental damage, lower operating costs, and preserve the supply of critical resources.

But, in 2026, as part of what EPA administrator Zeldin has called "the largest deregulatory action in U.S. history," - rolling back enforcement of dozens of environmental rules and inviting industrial facilities to apply for exemptions from pollution limits - the EPA has rescinded the "endangerment finding" which in turn signals an end, or at least severe weakening, to federal enforcement of emissions standards.

At the same time:

- Staffing at the EPA is being cut dramatically.
- Enforcement cases are being dropped.
- Research on the health impacts of air pollution is losing funding.
- The Department of Energy has announced it will stop enforcing dozens of environmental regulations.

When enforcement shrinks, pollution doesn't stop.

It increases. And its effects show up in emergency rooms.

What if you weren't sure that your water was safe to drink?

Who is making sure that our water is clean and healthy to drink? What kinds of things can be in the water that aren't good for you? I heard about what happened in Flint. But, there's no chance of that happening here, right?

Water is the most basic of human necessities. We're often told that one of the best things we can do for our health is to drink more of it. It's common to be offered water when you show up for an appointment, or a meeting, or anytime that you're a guest somewhere. *You* have probably offered your mailman, or contractor, or the friend who's dropping your kids off after a ball-game a glass of water on a hot day. And we all assume that the water is safe. All the time. Wherever we go in our country.

That is usually true because we have a long history of investment in public water treatment and delivery systems, ongoing research into contaminants that can get into water and how they affect our health, and monitoring of the water supply.

The Safe Drinking Water Act allows the EPA to set national limits on contaminants in public water systems. Those limits are updated when science identifies new risks — including PFAS, often called "forever chemicals," which have been linked to cancer and other serious illnesses. But right now, not only are regulations intended to limit exposure to PFAS being cut, so are our investments into *both* the infrastructure needed to keep public water supplies safe and the research that identifies contaminants in water.

You probably remember what happened in Flint, Michigan, all those children who got lead poisoning from improperly treated water and aged lead pipes. It made it very clear that we cannot put off replacing aging and lead public water infrastructure. But, the government is sending mixed messages with the EPA having promised new funding for lead pipe replacement in November of 2025 and then Congress voting to reduce funding for lead pipe replacement in Early 2026.

Keeping standards up to date also requires research. Monitoring water supplies requires funding and expertise. Enforcement requires staff. Billions in environmental and public health research grants have been terminated or frozen — including studies on PFAS, heat exposure, and airborne toxins.

What about cleaning up places that are already polluted?

Why is that rusted shell of an old factory still standing there with that big fence around it? How come there's nothing living in this pond? Why is that big area just outside of town all roped off? Generations of people in town have gotten sick from the pollution, why hasn't it been cleaned up?

Even as permits for polluting enterprises are being expedited and regulations loosened, the EPA claims to be more dedicated than ever to remediating the damage caused by past pollution. It is possible, even likely, that their focus could be shifting from prevention to remediation. But that's a tall order that requires adequate funding and staff.

There are more than 1,300 Superfund sites across the United States. These are places contaminated with highly dangerous things like toxic chemicals, pesticides, lead, and radioactive waste. Nearly 78 million Americans live within three miles of one of these sites.

Cleaning up Superfund sites takes years — sometimes decades — and costs billions. It requires commitment, steady investment, and deep expertise in the safe handling and disposal of toxic waste. The EPA's budget proposal would eliminate direct appropriations for Superfund, proposing instead to rely on tax and liability mechanisms.

What it could mean if cleanup slows:

- Contaminants continue leaching into soil and groundwater.
- Property values fall.
- Health risks accumulate.

Do you even know if your community sits near a former industrial dumping ground?

What if the farm upstream contaminates the river downstream?

Are the fish we caught safe to eat? Is the pond safe to swim in? Is this ground safe to build on?

Wetlands are not just a home for beavers, turtles, and mosquitoes. They are environmental workhorses. They filter pollution from water, soak up flood waters, and also support both scientifically and commercially important plants and animals.

Agriculture is one of the largest users of freshwater in the country. It is also a major source of runoff pollution — fertilizer, pesticides, animal waste — that flows into rivers and lakes. Wetlands, when protected, filter that runoff naturally.

But wetland protections are being weakened to the point where a majority of our wetlands may no longer be protected under the Clean Water Act. A rule proposed by the EPA would narrow the legal definition of "wetlands" so much that up to 90% of currently regulated wetlands could lose protection.

What if we stopped researching the environment?

What's the weather going to be like next week? There are always new chemicals or compounds that manufacturers claim are "safer" - how would we know if that were true? Is it really dangerous to sit out in the sun when it's hot out? How does anyone know which places are more likely to experience extreme weather?

Investment in environmental research has led to marvelous inventions and created a world where we have a stunning amount of information at our fingertips. We have long-term weather forecasts that are mostly accurate. We can map our entire country - or world - to see which areas are at risk of flooding or fire. We can identify an illness caused by exposure to a toxin vs one caused by a virus or bacteria. We can also follow a single whale on its journey around the world. We have invested in environmental research since the dawn of the nation, and we now have some of the most advanced environmental science organizations in the world -

The **National Oceanic and Atmospheric Administration** does far more than predict rain. It tracks atmospheric and oceanic systems that influence flooding, hurricanes, fisheries, and coastal erosion.

The **National Aeronautics and Space Administration** runs Earth-observing satellites that monitor ice melt, drought, wildfires, and air quality.

The **National Science Foundation** funds university research into climate, water systems, and environmental health.

The **National Institutes of Health** studies how environmental exposure affects human health.

But funding for all of these efforts is being cut or redirected. NSF has terminated climate and environmental justice research grants. NIH has ended future funding for research into the health effects of climate change. NASA's Earth Science budget faces nearly a 50% cut.

When this research stops:

- Early warnings disappear.
- Information gaps widen.
- Local governments plan blindly.
- Insurance markets destabilize.
- Disaster costs rise.

These cuts cut into our understanding of how our planet functions. You might not feel the loss of it tomorrow. You feel it when the flood maps are outdated.

When wildfire predictions are wrong. When heat deaths rise without explanation. When the house you thought would be high and dry for years gets washed away.

Why these cuts?

The EPA was created in 1970. President Nixon supported the founding of the agency as the right place to combine environmental research, oversight, and enforcement. The new agency was given one mission: To protect human health and the environment. And, we have seen remarkable improvements across our country as a result of the EPA's work. Waters too polluted to fish in are now great for fishing and swimming. Cities once engulfed in smog see the sun. Rare species of plants and animals have been brought back from the brink of extinction. And, the average fuel economy of new cars has doubled in the last 50 years. It is a success story.

But, in 2025, the EPA reframed its mission around "energy dominance", "permitting reform", and "economic growth". All of which are policy goals - even good ones for other government agencies - but they are not in line with the founding mission of the EPA: To protect human health and the environment.

Environmental protection does come with costs.

Compliance requires investment and innovation. But it isn't anti-business. You could argue that it protects the space and resources that we need to keep doing business in the long term. It exists because pollution has costs — costs to the health, wellbeing and longevity of humans.

Those costs don't disappear when the compliance burdens on companies are lessened. They shift. From the company to the town. From the regulators to parents. From prevention to higher healthcare costs.

Can't the States just set their own environmental standards?

What business is it of ours what they want to build on the other side of the country? What if the State just north of us builds a bunch of factories...right along the river? My State has good environmental laws - so nothing will change here, right?

The environment doesn't recognize boundaries. Winds blow and water flows between towns, states, and even countries year-round. That happens no matter what's in the air or water. So, even though every state has some environmental laws - six states even have a state constitutional right to a healthy environment - those laws don't protect your state from industrial farming run-off, wastewater dumpage, or emissions that come from other states. Protection from that came from the EPA setting and enforcing national standards.

But right now, not only is the EPA lowering standards, expediting permits, and cutting back on enforcement, the administration is also seeking to halt or minimize the enforcement of State environmental laws. The administration is cutting or withholding renewable energy funds and grants from States, the loss of which also costs jobs in states across the country.

Meanwhile, the administration and the DOJ are trying to minimize the state's ability to regulate emissions or prevent fossil fuel infrastructure from being built in their states. Ten states have legislation pending that would establish state-level environmental Superfunds, which would help them recover money from polluters to pay for damage done to the environment in the state. Two states already have such laws, but the DOJ is suing them, claiming that federal law preempts state law on the issue. This would leave states with little recourse to protect their citizens and environment as federal regulations are weakened. It would mean that States have to sit idly by as...

- Air pollution increases healthcare spending.
- Contaminated water reduces property values.
- Flooding drives up insurance premiums.
- Wildfires destabilize local economies.

- Toxic exposure increases long-term disability.

It also means that resources that are critical not only to our present security and economy, but also to our future, could be extracted from our environment much faster, leaving not only less clean air and water but also less of everything else that we need to raise, grow, and build in the future.

Bottom Line

The environment is our most critical resource.

The air you breathe.

The water you drink.

The land that grows your food.

These are not luxuries.

AFTERWORD

Hopefully this book shows that government is not abstract—it is embedded in daily life.

The chapters in this book aren't about policy—they're about *your home, your health, your commute, your kids.*

The government is not "out there." It is the system that makes modern life work. The danger is not just what gets cut. It's how quietly the system stops working. At first, nothing seems broken. Then something feels slower. Less reliable. Harder to access. More expensive. And then one day, something you assumed would be there… isn't.

How Cuts Actually Happen

When politicians talk about "cuts," most people imagine one simple thing: less money.

A program gets slashed. A line disappears from the budget. Something obvious shuts down.

But that's not how cuts usually work anymore.

Today, most of the damage doesn't come from dramatic shutdowns. It comes from quieter moves that are easier to deny, harder to track, and much more disruptive to everyday life. The result is the same—services weaken, costs rise, risks increase—but the cause is easier to hide.

Here are the five main ways cuts actually happen.

1. Budget Cuts: The Obvious One (and the Least Common)

This is the kind of cut people expect. Congress reduces funding for a program. An agency gets less money. Grants shrink. Services get reduced or eliminated. Sometimes the cut is direct. Other times it's sneakier: funding stays "flat" while costs rise. Inflation goes up, demand increases, but the budget doesn't. On paper, nothing changed. In real life, services quietly disappear. A program that helped ten families now helps six. A research grant that funded a full team now funds half a lab. A disaster fund that once lasted a full season runs dry halfway through.

This is the most visible kind of cut—but it's no longer the most common.

2. Staff Losses: When the Program Exists, but No One Is Left to Run It

You can't run public services without people. When agencies lose staff—through layoffs, hiring freezes, buyouts, or forced resignations—the program may still exist on paper, but it stops working in practice. Phones go unanswered. Inspections get skipped. Applications pile up. Reviews slow to a crawl. Emergencies take longer to respond to.

This is one of the easiest cuts to defend politically: "We didn't eliminate the program. It's still there." But if no one is left to answer the phone, enforce the rules, or deliver the help, the outcome is the same as a shutdown. Sometimes worse—because people keep applying, waiting, and relying on something that no longer functions.

3. Non-enforcement: The Rules Still Exist—They're Just Ignored

Another common move: keep the law, stop enforcing it.

Safety rules. Consumer protections. Environmental limits. Civil rights guarantees. Workplace standards. Airline rules. Housing protections. Instead of repealing them, agencies are told to:

- Stop investigating

- Stop auditing
- Stop penalizing violations
- "Use discretion"

This creates a dangerous illusion. People assume they're protected because the law still exists. But without enforcement, the rules become optional—especially for powerful companies.

When enforcement disappears:

- Unsafe behavior becomes cheaper
- Bad actors gain an advantage
- The public takes on more risk without knowing it

This is how protections vanish without a single vote.

4. Privatization: Turning Public Guarantees into Paid Services

Some cuts don't remove services. They turn them into products.

Instead of the government providing or guaranteeing something—disaster aid, forecasting, inspections, infrastructure—it gets handed to private companies. That changes everything.

Public services are designed to be:

- Universal
- Predictable
- Available when needed, not just when profitable

Private services are designed to:

- Make money
- Serve paying customers first
- Avoid high-risk or low-margin situations

When something is privatized, access often becomes uneven. Costs go up. Accountability goes down. And in emergencies—when profits disappear—so does the service. You don't lose the service all at once. You lose the guarantee.

5. Barriers to Access: Help Exists, But You Can't Reach It

This is the quietest cut of all. The program still exists. Funding might even still be there. But new rules make it harder—or impossible—to use. Common barriers include:

- More paperwork
- Shorter deadlines
- Fewer offices
- Online-only systems

- Stricter eligibility rules
- Confusing or constantly changing requirements

Each change sounds minor. Together, they push people out. Families miss deadlines. Small towns lose offices. Elderly people can't navigate online systems. Workers can't take time off to reapply. Immigrants avoid programs out of fear. The result is a "self-enforcing cut": fewer people get help, and officials point to declining usage as proof the program "isn't needed."

What You Can Do

Join us online at our website CutsCut.org to continue to build out, together, the impact of budget cuts at the federal level – and help us work through the specific impacts of these cuts at the state level for your community.

SOURCES

CHAPTER 1: YOUR HOME SWEET HOME

Consumer Financial Protection Bureau. (2024, July 11). Summary of 2023 data on mortgage lending. https://www.consumerfinance.gov/data-research/hmda/summary-of-2023-data-on-mortgage-lending/

Passmore, W., & Sherlund, S. M. (2016, April). FHA, Fannie Mae, Freddie Mac, and the Great Recession (Finance and Economics Discussion Series No. 2016-031). Board of Governors of the Federal Reserve System. https://www.federalreserve.gov/econres/feds/fha-fannie-mae-freddie-mac-and-the-great-recession.htm

U.S. Department of Housing and Urban Development. (2024). *Financial status of the FHA Mutual Mortgage Insurance Fund FY 2024.* https://www.hud.gov/sites/dfiles/Housing/documents/2024FHAAnnualReportMMIFund.pdf

Federal Deposit Insurance Corporation. (2024, August). U.S. Department of Agriculture. *Affordable Mortgage Lending Guide.* https://www.fdic.gov/system/files/2024-08/usda-overview.pdf

Birk, C. (2025, July 15). VA loan assumption: Breaking down how VA assumptions work. Veterans United Home Loans. https://www.veteransunited.com/valoans/va-loan-assumption/

Dettling, L. J., & Kearney, M. S. (2025, February). Did the modern mortgage set the stage for the U.S. baby boom? (Working Paper No. 33446). National Bureau of Economic Research. https://www.nber.org/papers/w33446

Bedayn, J. (2025, February 28). Trump administration to slash funding for enforcement of fair housing laws. *AP News.* https://apnews.com/article/trump-doge-housing-crisis-cuts-discrimination-d0c6e3b4b030787a1f60a7dc153153dd

U.S. Department of the Interior. (n.d.). Land and Water Conservation Fund. https://www.doi.gov/lwcf

Haggerty, M., & Rowland-Shea, J. (2025, February 20). Trump quietly plans to liquidate public lands to finance his sovereign wealth fund. *Center for American Progress.* https://www.american-progress.org/article/trump-quietly-plans-to-liquidate-public-lands-to-finance-his-sovereign-wealth-fund/

NOAA Office for Coastal Management. (2025, September 24). Economics and demographics. *Fast Facts.* https://coast.noaa.-gov/states/fast-facts/economics-and-demographics.html

Headwaters Economics. (2024, May 29). Updates to Wildfire Risk to Communities reveal 115 million people living with high wildfire risk. https://headwaterseconomics.org/natural-hazards/up-dates-to-wildfire-risk-to-communities/

FEMA. (Accessed May 29, 2025). Flood Maps. https://www.fe-ma.gov/flood-maps

Kennedy, B., Tyson, A., & Yam, E. (2024, July 23). Americans' extreme weather policy views and personal experiences. *Pew Research Center.* https://www.pewresearch.org/science/2024/07/23/americans-extreme-weather-policy-views-and-personal-experiences/

NOAA National Environmental Satellite, Data, and Information Service. (March 10, 2023). The Storm of the Century: A Look Back from NOAA Satellites. https://www.nesdis.noaa.gov/news/the-storm-of-the-century-look-back-noaa-satellites#:~:text=Whether%2520you%2520-call%2520it%2520the,the%2520nation%252030%2520years%2520ago

Olivia of Troy. (May 6, 2025). The Storm is Coming. FEMA Isn't. https://www.livingitwitholiviatroye.com/p/the-storm-is-coming-fema-isnt

Kochhar, R., & Moslimani, M. (2023, December 4). The assets households own and the debts they carry. Pew Research Center. https://www.pewresearch.org/2023/12/04/the-assets-households-own-and-the-debts-they-carry/#:~:text=An%20owned%20primary%20residence%20and,other%20assets%20stood%20at%20$20%2C000

Corfidi, S. (2010, February 13). A brief history of the Storm Prediction Center. National Weather Service Storm Prediction Center. https://www.spc.noaa.gov/history/early.html

Hagen, A. B., Cangialosi, J. P., Chenard, M., Alaka, L., & Delgado, S. (2025, April 8). Hurricane Helene (AL092024) 24–27 September 2024: Tropical cyclone report. National Hurricane Center. https://www.nhc.noaa.gov/data/tcr/AL092024_Helene.pdf

NOAA National Centers for Environmental Information. (2025). Billion-dollar weather and climate disasters: Time series. U.S. Billion-Dollar Weather and Climate Disasters. https://www.ncei.noaa.gov/access/billions/time-series

Garratt, D., & Stark, J. W. (2009, February 25). Post Katrina disaster response and recovery: Evaluating FEMA's continuing efforts in the Gulf Coast and response to recent disasters [Congressional testimony]. Federal Emergency Management Agency, Department of Homeland Security. https://www.fema.gov/pdf/about/testimony/022509_testimony.pdf

The White House. (2008, August 20). Fact sheet: Rebuilding the Gulf Coast. George W. Bush White House Archives. https://georgewbush-whitehouse.archives.gov/infocus/katrina/

CHAPTER 2: YOUR HEALTHCARE

American Academy of Pediatrics. (2025, February 27). AAP analysis: 49% of children insured by Medicaid or CHIP. *AAP News*. https://publications.aap.org/aapnews/news/31491/AAP-analysis-49-of-children-insured-by-Medicaid-or?autologincheck=redirected

Perrone, M. (2025, May 16). FDA OKs first blood test that can help diagnose Alzheimer's disease. *AP News*. https://apnews.com/article/alzheimers-blood-test-fda-leqembi-kisunla-ad3cffe0b-d540accf47e8ee105b439a9

Centers for Disease Control and Prevention. (2023, June 26). CDC timeline 1990s. David J. Sencer CDC Museum. https://www.cdc.gov/museum/timeline/1990.html

Centers for Medicare & Medicaid Services. (2025). Medicare monthly enrollment [Dataset]. U.S. Department of Health and Human Services. https://data.cms.gov/summary-statistics-on-beneficiary-enrollment/medicare-and-medicaid-reports/medicare-monthly-enrollment/data

Jenco, M. (2026, January 7). 2025 measles cases highest since 1991. AAP News. https://publications.aap.org/aapnews/news/34124/2025-measles-cases-highest-since-1991

Sy, S., & Norris, C. (2026, January 23). Measles cases surged in 2025 as vaccination rates dropped. PBS NewsHour. https://www.pbs.org/newshour/show/measles-cases-surged-in-2025-as-vaccination-rates-dropped

Splete, H. (2026, January 6). CDC cuts recommended childhood vaccines to 11. Medscape Medical News. https://www.medscape.com/viewarticle/cdc-cuts-recommended-childhood-vaccines-11-2026a10000ax?form=fpf

U.S. Department of Health and Human Services. (2026, January 5). CDC acts on presidential memorandum to update childhood immunization schedule [Press release]. https://www.hhs.gov/press-room/cdc-acts-presidential-memorandum-update-childhood-immunization-schedule.html

American Hospital Association. (2022, May). *Fact sheet: Majority hospital payments dependent on Medicare or Medicaid; Congress continues to cut hospital reimbursements for Medicare*. https://www.aha.org/system/files/media/file/2022/05/fact-sheet-majority-hospital-payments-dependent-on-medicare-or-medicaid-congress-continues-to-cut-hospital-reimbursements-for-medicare.pdf

Kane, L. (2025, August 22). Should you drop Medicare? Payment cuts continue to strain medical practices, and many doctors have toyed with the idea of opting out. How to decide. MedCentral. https://www.medcentral.com/biz-policy/should-you-drop-medicare

Congressional Budget Office. (2025, May 20). Potential statutory pay-as-you-go effects of a bill to provide reconciliation pursuant to H. Con. Res. 14, the One Big Beautiful Bill Act [Letter to Honorable Brendan F. Boyle]. https://www.cbo.gov/system/files/2025-05/61423-PAYGO.pdf

Goldman, M. (2025, April 29). *Exclusive: Where nursing homes rely most on Medicaid*. Axios. https://www.axios.com/2025/04/29/state-nursing-homes-medicaid-data

UPDATED: Nearly 600 nursing homes named at high risk of closure if Medicaid cuts approved. (2025, July 4). McKnight's Long-Term Care

News. https://www.mcknights.com/news/breaking-nearly-600-nursing-homes-at-risk-of-closure-if-medicaid-cuts-approved/

Wyden, R., Warner, M., Merkley, J., & Schumer, C. (2025, June 27). *Wyden, Warner, Merkley and Schumer highlight threat to nursing homes if GOP approves Medicaid cuts. United States Senate Committee on Finance.* https://www.finance.senate.gov/ranking-members-news/wyden-warner-merkley-and-schumer-highlight-threat-to-nursing-homes-if-gop-approves-medicaid-cuts

CHAPTER 3: YOUR TRANSPORTATION

Potter, B. (2024, November 20). *How Good Are American Roads?* Construction-Physics.com; Construction Physics. https://www.construction-physics.com/p/how-good-are-american-roads

Fact file: Americans drive the most. (2022, August 6). Frontier Group. https://frontiergroup.org/resources/fact-file-americans-drive-most/

American Society of Civil Engineers. (2025). *Executive summary: A comprehensive assessment of America's infrastructure.* https://infrastructurereportcard.org/wp-content/uploads/2025/03/Executive-Summary-2025-Natl-IRC-WEB.pdf

McGeehan, P. (2026, January 27). Work will stop on critical tunnel project unless Trump restores funding. The New York Times. https://www.nytimes.com/2026/01/27/nyregion/hudson-tunnel-gateway-funding.html

Federal Highway Administration. (2023, August 8). *History of the Interstate Highway System.* U.S. Department of Transportation. https://highways.dot.gov/highway-history/interstate-system/50th-anniversary/history-interstate-highway-system

Salerno, C. (2025, February 6). *Unflooding the zone: What do the Trump administration's latest actions signal for transportation? - Transporta-*

tion For America. Transportation for America. https://t4america.org/2025/02/05/unflooding-the-zone-what-do-the-trump-administrations-latest-actions-signal-for-transportation/

Jeans-Gail, S. (2025, October 10). USDOT funding freeze for rail mega-projects drags on. Rail Passengers Association. https://www.railpassengers.org/happening-now/news/blog/usdot-funding-freeze-for-rail-mega-projects-drags-on/

Air Traffic By The Numbers | Federal Aviation Administration. (2024). Faa.gov. https://www.faa.gov/air_traffic/by_the_numbers

Bureau of Transportation Statistics. (n.d.). Search airline employment data by month. U.S. Department of Transportation. https://www.transtats.bts.gov/employment/

Amtrak. (2024, April 18). FY 2023 company profile: For the period October 1, 2022 - September 30, 2023. https://www.amtrak.com/content/dam/projects/dotcom/english/public/documents/corporate/nationalfactsheets/Amtrak-Company-Profile-FY2023-041824.pdf

American Society of Civil Engineers. (2025). Rail. *2025 Infrastructure Report Card*. https://infrastructurereportcard.org/cat-item/rail-infrastructure/

DeGood, K. (2015, June 4). Understanding Amtrak and the importance of passenger rail in the United States. *Center for American Progress*. https://www.americanprogress.org/article/understanding-amtrak-and-the-importance-of-passenger-rail-in-the-united-states/

NBC New York Staff. (2024, July 8). It's so hot that an NYC bridge literally stopped working. *NBC New York*. Updated July 9, 2024. https://www.nbcnewyork.com/news/its-so-hot-that-a-nyc-bridge-literally-stopped-working/5576418/

U.S. Environmental Protection Agency. (2026, February 12). President Trump and Administrator Zeldin deliver single largest deregulatory action in U.S. history. https://www.epa.gov/newsreleases/president-trump-and-administrator-zeldin-deliver-single-largest-deregulatory-action-us

Ewing, R. (2025, May 5). Trump looks to slash Essential Air Service program. *AirlineGeeks.* https://airlinegeeks.com/2025/05/05/trump-looks-to-slash-essential-air-service-program/

Shapero, J. (2025, March 7). Musk's SpaceX confirms Starlink lease agreement with FAA. *The Hill.* https://thehill.com/policy/technology/5182848-musks-spacex-confirms-starlink-lease-agreement-with-faa/

Brookings Institution. (2025, September 30). Tracking regulatory changes in the second Trump administration. *Brookings.* https://www.brookings.edu/articles/tracking-regulatory-changes-in-the-second-trump-administration/

Roberson, J. E. (2025, February 3). Department of Transportation issues sweeping changes to policies and programs. Holland & Knight. https://www.hklaw.com/en/insights/publications/2025/02/department-of-transportation-issues-sweeping-changes

U.S. Department of Transportation. (2025, January 29). Implementation of Executive Orders Addressing Energy, Climate Change, Diversity, and Gender [Memorandum].

Federal Aviation Administration. (2025, May 8). U.S. Transportation Secretary Sean P. Duffy unveils plan to build brand new, state-of-the-art air traffic control system. *U.S. Department of Transportation.* https://www.faa.gov/newsroom/us-transportation-secretary-sean-p-duffy-unveils-plan-build-brand-new-state-art-air

The White House. (2025, May 8). ICYMI: Trump Administration's plan to modernize air traffic control system. https://www.whitehouse.gov/articles/2025/05/icymi-trump-administrations-plan-to-modernize-air-traffic-control-system/

Shepardson, D., & Singh, R. K. (2025, May 8). Trump's plan to fix air traffic control faces huge hurdles. *Reuters*. https://www.reuters.com/business/aerospace-defense/trumps-plan-fix-air-traffic-control-faces-huge-hurdles-2025-05-08/

Shepardson, D., & Hunnicutt, T. (2025, April 30). Trump says IBM, Raytheon may get US contract to modernize air traffic control system. *Reuters*. https://www.reuters.com/business/aerospace-defense/trump-says-ibm-raytheon-might-get-contract-modernize-air-traffic-controller-2025-04-30/

CHAPTER 4: YOUR EDUCATION

Supreme Court of the United States. (2025, July 14). McMahon v. New York, No. 24A1203 (Order granting stay; dissenting opinion of Justice Sotomayor). https://www.supremecourt.gov/opinions/24pdf/24a1203_new_6j37.pdf

Food Research & Action Center. (2025, July 1). Senate passes disastrous budget bill, FRAC urges House to stop dangerous SNAP cuts. FRAC. https://frac.org/news/senatevotejuly25#:~:text=Cuts%20to%20SNAP%20will%20also,students%20through%20the%20Community%20Eligibility

Aikens, N., Atkins-Burnett, S., Tarullo, L., Malone, L., Kelly, A., & Cannon, J. (2020). Preschool boys of color: Portraits of the population served by Head Start. Journal of Applied Developmental Psychology, 70, 101167. https://doi.org/10.1016/j.appdev.2020.101167

Available at: https://www.sciencedirect.com/science/article/abs/pii/S0193397320301593#:~:text=Introduction,of%20Head%20Start%20%282018%29

Hanson, M. (2024, November 25). Economic effects of student loan debt. EducationData.org. https://educationdata.org/student-loan-debt-economic-impact

Waldman, A., & Lerner, S. (2025, March 24). NIH ends future funding to study the health effects of climate change. ProPublica. https://www.propublica.org/article/nih-funding-climate-change-public-health

Knott, K. (2025, May 2). What Trump's proposed budget cuts mean for education, research. Inside Higher Ed. https://www.inside-highered.com/news/government/student-aid-policy/2025/05/02/trump-proposes-deep-cuts-education-and-research

Cohn, J. (2025, May 8). How much federal funding do colleges and universities receive? Urban Wire. Urban Institute. https://www.urban.org/urban-wire/how-much-federal-funding-do-colleges-and-universities-receive

Zampini, M. (2025, May 6). House Republicans propose slashing Pell Grants. The Institute for College Access & Success. https://ticas.org/affordability-2/pell-grants-reconciliation-2025/

Desjean, J. (2025, May 5). Reconciliation deep dive: House Committee proposes major changes to Pell Grant, campus-based aid, need-analysis, and student eligibility. NASFAA. https://www.nasfaa.org/news-item/36197/Reconciliation_Deep_Dive_House_Committee_Proposes_Major_Changes_to_Pell_Grant_Campus-Based_Aid_Need-Analysis_and_Student_Eligibility

Hanson, M. (2024, November 3). Pell grant statistics. EducationData.org. https://educationdata.org/pell-grant-statistics

Walter, M. (2025, May 6). Reconciliation deep dive: House Committee proposes major overhaul of federal student loans, repayment, and PSLF. NASFAA.

The White House. (2025, March 7). Restoring public service loan forgiveness. https://www.whitehouse.gov/presidential-actions/2025/03/restoring-public-service-loan-forgiveness/

Bennett, G., & Cuevas, K. (2025, December 3). Proposal to declassify nursing as 'professional' threatens ability to secure student loans. PBS NewsHour. https://www.pbs.org/newshour/show/proposal-to-declassify-nursing-as-professional-threatens-ability-to-secure-student-loans

National Nurses United. (2026, February 4). Nurses condemn proposed rule, now up for public comment, capping graduate nursing student loans [Press release]. https://www.nationalnursesunited.org/press/nurses-condemn-proposed-rule-capping-graduate-nursing-student-loans

House Committee on Education and the Workforce. (2024). Providing for reconciliation pursuant to H.Con.Res. 14, the Concurrent Resolution on the Budget for Fiscal Year 2025: Section-by-section (PDF). https://edworkforce.house.gov/path/to/document.pdf

U.S. Department of Education, National Center for Education Statistics. (2023, August). Postsecondary institution revenues. In Digest of Education Statistics. https://nces.ed.gov/programs/coe/indicator/cud/postsecondary-institution-revenue

Cohn, J. (2025, May 8). How much federal funding do colleges and universities receive? Urban Institute. https://www.urban.org/urban-wire/how-much-federal-funding-do-colleges-and-universities-receive

Hanson, M. (2025, August 8). Student loan debt statistics. Education Data Initiative. https://educationdata.org/student-loan-debt-statistics

Urban Institute. (n.d.). Borrowing: By student characteristics. College Affordability and Completion. https://collegeaffordability.urban.org/covering-expenses/borrowing/#/by_student_characteristics

Board of Governors of the Federal Reserve System. (2025, June 12). Higher education and student loans. In Report on the Economic Well-Being of U.S. Households in 2024. https://www.federalreserve.gov/publications/2025-economic-well-being-of-us-households-in-2024-higher-education-and-student-loans.htm#:~:text=79,than%20$25%2C000%20(table%2044).

DeSilver, D. (2025, March 18). What the data says about the U.S. Department of Education. Pew Research Center. https://www.pewresearch.org/short-reads/2025/03/18/what-the-data-says-about-the-us-department-of-education/#which-states-and-cities-rely-most-on-federal-funding-for-local-public-k-12-schools

Skinner, R. R., Smole, D. P., & Stoll, A. (2024, December 12). A summary of federal education laws administered by the U.S. Department of Education (CRS In Focus No. IF10551). Congressional Research Service. https://www.congress.gov/crs-product/IF10551

United States District Court for the District of Massachusetts. (2025, May 22). Memorandum and order on consolidated plaintiffs' motions for preliminary injunction (Civil Action Nos. 25-10601-MJJ & 25-10677-MJJ) (Doc. No. 45). Retrieved from https://storage.courtlistener.com/recap/gov.uscourts.mad.282419/gov.uscourts.mad.282419.45.0.pdf

Howe, A. (2025, July 14). Supreme Court clears the way for Trump administration to massively reduce the size of the Department of Education. SCOTUSblog. https://www.scotusblog.com/2025/07/supreme-court-clears-the-way-for-trump-administration-to-massively-reduce-the-size-of-the-department-of-education/

Booth, L. (2025, February 14). Can the president dismantle the Department of Education by executive order? Just Security. https://www.justsecurity.org/107918/dismantle-department-education-executive-order/

Hanacek, A. (2025, March 11). USDA, DOGE slash about $1 billion in school nutrition funding programs. Food Processing. https://www.foodprocessing.com/business-of-food-beverage/legal-issues/news/55273944/usda-doge-slash-about-1-billion-in-school-nutrition-funding-programs

School Nutrition Association. (2025, March 10). Proposed school meal cuts prompt nationwide advocacy. School Nutrition Association. https://schoolnutrition.org/sna-news/proposed-school-meal-cuts-prompt-nationwide-advocacy/

Food Research & Action Center. (n.d.). National School Lunch Program. FRAC. Retrieved October 1, 2025, from https://frac.org/programs/national-school-lunch-program#:~:text=Quick%20-Facts:%20*%20Just%20over%2028%20million,participate%20in%20the%20National%20School%20Lunch%20Program

Peter G. Peterson Foundation. (2025, July 22). How is K-12 education funded? Retrieved October 1, 2025, from https://www.pgpf.org/article/how-is-k-12-education-funded/

National Head Start Association. (2025, May 2). Statement from the National Head Start Association on White House budget recommendations. https://nhsa.org/press_release/statement-from-the-national-head-start-association-on-white-house-budget-recommendations/

Gecker, J. (2025, April 17). White House proposes eliminating Head Start funding as part of sweeping budget cuts. Associated Press. https://apnews.com/article/head-start-trump-funding-budget-cuts-education-204077e046329eb22c71445d57ba002b

Mumphrey, C. (2025, April 16). Head Start funding lags by nearly $1 billion this year, causing some preschool closures. AP News. https://apnews.com/article/head-start-funding-preschool-child-care-closures-1f92fa98f320c7c14db63e69b986d11d

Administration for Children and Families, U.S. Department of Health and Human Services. (2025, February 27). Head Start program facts: Fiscal year 2022. HeadStart.gov. https://headstart.gov/program-data/article/head-start-program-facts-fiscal-year-2022

CHAPTER 5: YOUR MEALS

Ketpal,V. STAT. (2025, March 10). *Trump tariffs may raise prices on produce and avocados.* https://www.statnews.com/2025/03/10/trump-tariffs-diet-grocery-prices-produce-avocados-mexico/

Mahoney, C.J. (2025, March 5). *Back to the brink: North American trade in the 2nd Trump administration.* Brookings Institution. https://www.brookings.edu/articles/back-to-the-brink-north-american-trade-in-the-2nd-trump-administration/

Edwards, C. (2023, August 31). *Cutting federal farm subsidies* (Briefing Paper No. 195). Cato Institute. https://www.cato.org/briefing-paper/cutting-federal-farm-subsidies#types-farm-subsidy

Wadykah, S. (2025, January 21). *Is it okay to eat some processed foods?* Consumer Reports. https://www.consumerreports.org/health/packaged-processed-foods/is-it-okay-to-eat-some-processed-foods-a8560741913/

O'Niell Hayes, T., Kerska, K. (2021, November 3). *A primer on agricul-*

ture subsidies and their influence on the composition of U.S. food supply and consumption. American Action Forum. https://www.americanactionforum.org/research/primer-agriculture-subsidies-and-their-influence-on-the-composition-of-u-s-food-supply-and-consumption/

Zahniser, S. (2025, January, 16). Fruit and vegetable imports [Chart of note]._ U.S. Department of Agriculture, Economic Research Service. https://www.ers.usda.gov/data-products/charts-of-note/chart-detail?chartId=110713

Environmental Working Group. (n.d.). *Total subsidies by state, 1995–2024 — The United States.* Farm Subsidy Database. https://farm.ewg.org/progdetail.php?fips=00000&progcode=total&page=states&regionname=theUnitedStates

Economic Research Service, U.S. Department of Agriculture. (2025, April 1). *Agricultural trade. Ag and food statistics: Charting the essentials.* https://www.ers.usda.gov/data-products/ag-and-food-statistics-charting-the-essentials/agricultural-trade

Harvesters Community Food Network. (2025, June 4). One Big, Beautiful Bill: What does it mean for SNAP and Medicaid? https://www.harvesters.org/one-big-beautiful-bill-what-does-it-mean-for-snap-and-medicaid

U.S. Department of Agriculture, Food and Nutrition Service. *SNAP retailer management dashboard*. Retrieved September 26, 2025, from https://www.fns.usda.gov/data-research/data-visualization/snap-retailer-management-dashboard

Tax Policy Center. (2025, May 20). *How would potential federal budget cuts impact state budgets?* https://taxpolicycenter.org/features/how-would-potential-federal-budget-cuts-impact-state-budgets.

Bergh, K., Rosenbaum, D., Tharp, W. (2025, May 28). *House reconciliation bill proposes deepest SNAP cut in history, would take food from millions of poor people.* Center on Budget and Policy Priorities. https://www.cbpp.org/research/food-assistance/house-reconciliation-bill-proposes-deepest-snap-cut-in-history-would-take

Center on Budget and Policy Priorities. (2024, November 25). *The Supplemental Nutrition Assistance Program (SNAP).* https://www.cbpp.org/research/food-assistance/the-supplemental-nutrition-assistance-program-snap

Gutelius, B., Pinto, S. (2024, May 20). *Handling hardship: Understanding the challenges of financial stress.* University of Illinois Chicago, Center for Urban Economic Development. https://indigo.uic.edu/articles/report/Handling_Hardship_Data_on_Economic_Insecurity_Among_Amazon_Warehouse_Workers/25823068?file=46334659

U.S. Government Accountability Office. (2020, October 19). *Food assistance: Data on work requirements and time limits for the Supplemental Nutrition Assistance Program* (GAO-21-45). https://www.gao.gov/products/gao-21-45

Jeffrey, J., & Yelenik, M. (2025, July 18). MAP: *See How Cuts to SNAP Food Assistance Affect Your State.* U.S. News & World Report. https://www.usnews.com/news/national-news/articles/2025-05-22/map-see-how-cuts-to-snap-food-assistance-would-affect-your-state

Cespedes, A., & Dorn, S. (2025, February 24). *The House Budget Resolution's cuts to SNAP would be the largest in U.S. history.* UnidosUS. https://unidosus.org/blog/2025/02/24/house-budget-resolutions-cuts-to-snap-largest-in-us-history/

US Department of Agriculture. *Barriers that Constrain the Adequacy of SNAP Allotments* | Food and Nutrition Service. (n.d.) www.fns.usda.gov. https://www.fns.usda.gov/research/snap/barriers-constrain-adequacy-allotments

U.S. Department of Agriculture, Center for Nutrition Policy and Promotion. (2021). *The thrifty food plan, 2021.* https://www.fns.usda.gov/cnpp/thrifty-food-plan-2021

Personal Responsibility and Work Opportunity Reconciliation Act of 1996, Pub. L. No. 104-193. (1996, August 22)). https://www.govinfo.gov/content/pkg/PLAW-104publ193/html/PLAW-104publ193.htm

Hartline-Grafton, H., Advisor, S., SNAP, Vollinger, E., & Director, L.

S. (n.d.). *Thrifty Food Plan 101 (Part 1).* Food Research & Action Center. https://frac.org/blog/thrifty-food-plan-101-part-1

Center on Budget and Policy Priorities. (2024, September 30). *A Quick Guide to SNAP Eligibility and Benefits.* Center on Budget and Policy Priorities. https://www.cbpp.org/research/food-assistance/a-quick-guide-to-snap-eligibility-and-benefits

U.S. Department of Agriculture, Economic Research Service. (2025, July 24). *Supplemental Nutrition Assistance Program (SNAP) - Key statistics and research.* https://www.ers.usda.gov/topics/food-nutrition-assistance/supplemental-nutrition-assistance-program-snap/key-statistics-research/

Rabbitt, M. P., Reed-Jones, M., Hales, L. J., & Burke, M. P. (2024). *Statistical supplement to household food security in the United States in 2023* (Report No. AP-124). U.S. Department of Agriculture, Economic Research Service. https://doi.org/10.32747/2024.8753946.ers

Karsit, I. (2023, December 27). *Healthy foods are often more expensive. Here's why.* CNBC. https://www.cnbc.com/2023/12/27/healthy-foods-are-often-more-expensive-heres-why.html

U.S. Bureau of Labor Statistics. (2025, September 11). *Consumer Price Index for All Urban Consumers: Food at Home in U.S. City Average* [CUSR0000SAF11]. FRED, Federal Reserve Bank of St. Louis. https://fred.stlouisfed.org/series/CUSR0000SAF11

Center on Budget and Policy Priorities. (2025, January 21). *SNAP: State by state data, fact sheets, and resources.* https://www.cbpp.org/research/food-assistance/snap-state-by-state-data-fact-sheets-and-resources

Food Safety, Inspection and Regulation

The Associated Press. (2024, October 15). USDA launches internal investigation into Boar's Head outbreak. *VPM News.*

https://www.vpm.org/news/2024/10/15/usda-launches-internal-investigation-into-boars-head-outbreak

U.S. Department of Agriculture, Food Safety and Inspection Service. (2025, January 10). Review of the Boar's Head Listeria monocytogenes outbreak - January 2025. https://www.fsis.usda.gov/news-events/publications/review-boars-head-listeria-monocytogenes-outbreak-january-2025

Top Class Actions. (2025, April 3). *$3.1M Boar's Head meat recall class action settlement.* https://topclassactions.com/lawsuit-settlements/closed-settlements/3-1m-boars-head-listeria-contamination-class-action-settlement/

Food Safety and Inspection Service. (2022, October 4). *States with and without inspection programs.* U.S. Department of Agriculture. https://www.fsis.usda.gov/inspection/state-inspection-programs/states-and-without-inspection-programs

McCarthy, R. (2025, March 7). *Trump administration eliminating two food safety committees.* Meat + Poultry. https://www.meatpoultry.com/articles/31581-trump-administration-eliminating-two-food-safety-committees

Henderson, B., & Blume, A. (2025, December 26). A 2025 timeline of U.S. federal food safety changes under the Trump admin. Food Safety Magazine. https://www.food-safety.com/articles/11004-a-2025-timeline-of-us-federal-food-safety-changes-under-the-trump-admin

Katz, E. (2025, April 2). *Some USDA RIF plans take shape as department warns employees of major cuts.* Government Executive. https://www.govexec.com/management/2025/04/some-usda-rif-plans-take-shape-department-warns-employees-major-cuts/404247/

Khimm, S. (2025, May 9). FDA stalls in posting food safety warning letters amid staff cuts. NBC News. https://www.nbcnews.com/health/health-news/fda-stalls-posting-food-safety-warning-letters-staff-cuts-rcna204879

Noguchi, Y. (2025, May 29). *How safe is the food supply after federal cutbacks? Experts are worried.* NPR. https://www.npr.org/sections/shots-health-news/2025/05/29/nx-s1-5413449/food-safety-inspection-fda-usda

FoodDocs. (2021, October 29). *What is HACCP certification? Your golden ticket to staying in business.* FoodDocs. https://www.fooddocs.com/post/what-is-haccp-certification

Beach, C. (2025, April 14). *Salmonella testing program for some chicken products on hold for 6 months.* Food Safety News. https://www.foodsafetynews.com/2025/04/salmonella-testing-program-for-some-chicken-products-on-hold-for-6-months/

Food Safety and Inspection Service. (n.d.). *Our history.* U.S. Department of Agriculture. https://www.fsis.usda.gov/about fsis/history

Thatte, D. (2019, October 17). *The Food Safety Modernization Act in a nutshell.* Manufacturing Innovation Blog. National Institute of Standards and Technology. https://www.nist.gov/blogs/manufacturing-innovation/food-safety-modernization-act-nutshell

U.S. Food and Drug Administration. (2019, February 13). *Investigation summary: Factors potentially contributing to the contamination of romaine lettuce implicated in the Fall 2018 multi-state outbreak of E. coli* O157:H7. https://www.fda.gov/food/outbreaks-foodborne-illness/investigation-summary-factors-potentially-contributing-contamination-romaine-lettuce-implicated-fall

Editorial Team. (2025, May 5). *More than 15,000 USDA employees take Trump Administration's resignation offer.* Food Safety Magazine.

https://www.food-safety.com/articles/10361-more-than-15-000-usda-employees-take-trump-administrations-resignation-offer

Califf, R. M. (2023, March 30). *The U.S. has one of the safest food supplies in the world*. FDA Voices. U.S. Food and Drug Administration.
https://www.fda.gov/news-events/fda-voices/us-has-one-safest-food-supplies-world

The Economist Group. (2022). *Global Food Security Index 2022: Global report*. Economist Impact. https://impact.economist.com/sustainability/project/food-security-index/reports/Economist_Impact_GFSI_2022_Global_Report_Sep_2022.pdf

Karsit, I. (2023, December 27). *Healthy foods are often more expensive. Here's why*. CNBC. https://www.cnbc.com/2023/12/27/healthy-foods-are-often-more-expensive-heres-why.html

U.S. Department of Agriculture, Food Safety and Inspection Service. (2024, September 26). *Understanding FSIS food recalls*. https://www.fsis.usda.gov/food-safety/safe-food-handling-and-preparation/food-safety-basics/understanding-fsis-food-recalls

Centers for Disease Control and Prevention. (2024, May 2). *CDC and food safety*. https://www.cdc.gov/food-safety/about/what-cdc-is-doing.html

U.S. Food and Drug Administration. (2025, September 9). *Fees under the FDA Food Safety Modernization Act (FSMA)*. https://www.fda.gov/food/food-safety-modernization-act-fsma/fees-under-fsma

U.S. Government Accountability Office. (2025, February 3) *Food safety: Status of Foodborne Illness in the US*. GAO-25-107606. https://www.gao.gov/assets/880/875771.pdf
The Economist Group. (2022). *Global Food Security Index 2022: Global report*. Economist Impact. https://impact.economist.com/sus-

tainability/project/food-security-index/reports/Economist_Impact_GFSI_2022_Global_Report_Sep_2022.pdf

Karsit, I. (2023, December 27). *Healthy foods are often more expensive. Here's why*. CNBC. https://www.cnbc.com/2023/12/27/healthy-foods-are-often-more-expensive-heres-why.html

U.S. Food and Drug Administration. (2024, February 5). *Food Safety Modernization Act (FSMA).* U.S. Department of Health and Human Services. https://www.fda.gov/food/guidance-regulation-food-and-dietary-supplements/food-safety-modernization-act-fsma

CHAPTER 6: YOUR SECURITY

Insinna, V. (2025, September 17). *House narrowly passes reconciliation bill with $150B for* (FEMA, n.d.)*defense*. Breaking Defense. https://breakingdefense.com/2025/05/house-narrowly-passes-reconciliation-bill-with-150b-for-defense/

Kaste, M. (2025, May 24). Justice Department cuts to public safety grants leave police and nonprofits scrambling. https://www.npr.org/2025/05/24/nx-s1-5392378/justice-department-cuts-to-public-safety-grants-leave-police-and-nonprofits-scrambling

Anderson, M. (2025, November 10). Public safety groups face an uncertain future months after federal grant cuts. NPR. https://www.npr.org/2025/11/10/nx-s1-5552704/doj-crime-prevention-public-safety-grant-cuts

Brownlee, C. (2026, January 21). Trump has slashed federal funding for gun violence prevention. But how much exactly? The Trace. https://www.thetrace.org/2026/01/trump-public-safety-gun-violence-funding/

FEMA.gov. (2025, April 4). FEMA Ends Wasteful, Politicized Grant Program, Returning Agency to Core Mission of Helping Americans

Recovering from Natural Disasters. https://web.archive.org/web/20250426001312/https://www.fema.gov/press-release/20250404/fema-ends-wasteful-politicized-grant-program-returning-agency-core-mission

Federal Environmental Justice Tracker, Harvard Law School. (2025, August 6). *President Trump, FEMA terminated programs to address vulnerable communities' disaster risk. https://eelp.law.harvard.edu/tracker/fema-issued-new-building-resilient-infrastructure-and-communities-bric-policy/*

Solomon, A. (2025, May 29). *DOJ funding Update: A deeper look at the cuts - Council on Criminal Justice.* Council on Criminal Justice. https://counciloncj.org/doj-funding-update-a-deeper-look-at-the-cuts/

Amaning, A., & Preston, A. (2025, May 5). *The Trump administration's unprecedented cuts to DOJ grants undermine public safety.* Center for American Progress. https://www.americanprogress.org/article/the-trump-administrations-unprecedented-cuts-to-doj-grants-undermine-public-safety/

Hughes, W. (2022, December 28). *Guard saved lives, property responding to 2022 disasters.* National Guard. https://www.nationalguard.mil/News/Article-View/Article/3255837/guard-saved-lives-property-responding-to-2022-disasters/

Curran-Groome, W., Rumbach, A., & McTarnaghan, S. (2025, April 18). *FEMA is eliminating hazard mitigation programs, leaving Americans nationwide at risk as disasters worsen.* Urban Institute. *https://www.urban.org/urban-wire/fema-eliminating-hazard-mitigation-programs-leaving-americans-nationwide-risk-disasters#:~:text=The%20Federal%20Emergency%20Management%20Agency,%28FMA%29%20funding%20for%202025*

Ross, H. (2025, May 5). *Senators warn FEMA cuts will harm disaster mitigation, raise insurance costs.* S&P Global Market Intelligence.

https://www.spglobal.com/market-intelligence/en/news-insights/articles/2025/5/senators-warn-fema-cuts-will-harm-disaster-mitigation-raise-insurance-costs-88672123

Statista. (2025, January 27). *U.S. military force numbers 2023, by service branch and reserve component. https://www.statista.com/statistics/232330/us-military-force-numbers-by-service-branch-and-reserve-component/*

Nunn, J. (2025, June 10). *The Posse Comitatus Act explained.* Brennan Center for Justice. *https://www.brennancenter.org/our-work/research-reports/posse-comitatus-act-explained#:~:text=No%2C%20only%20federal%20military%20personnel,are%20returned%20to%20state%20control*

Navarro, M. (2024, February 15). *The Insurrection Act is a presidential power that threatens democracy.* Brennan Center for Justice. https://www.brennancenter.org/our-work/analysis-opinion/insurrection-act-presidential-power-threatens-democracy

Copp, T., & Santana, R. (2025, May 16). *DHS asks for 20,000 National Guard troops for immigration roundups | AP News.* AP News. *https://apnews.com/article/national-guard-troops-immigration-dhs-raids-8cbec5b0872a57b594fd75dce57f4dd0*

Freedman, A. (2025, July 13). *Texas NWS office had no warning coordination meteorologist during the flood. Did it make a difference?* CNN. *https://www.cnn.com/2025/07/13/weather/texas-flooding-nws-meteorologist-missing-climate*

Hernandez, J. (2025, July 6). *How good was the Texas weather forecast before the flood?* NPR. https://www.npr.org/2025/07/06/nx-s1-5458512/texas-flash-flood-weather-forecast

Joselow, M. (2025, July 11). *FEMA Didn't Answer Thousands of Calls From Flood Survivors, Documents Show.* The New York Times. https://www.nytimes.com/2025/07/11/climate/fema-missed-calls-texas-floods.html

Lee, T. F. M. (2025, July 15). *Texas failed to spend federal aid for disaster protection*. E&E News by POLITICO. *https://www.eenews.net/articles/texas-failed-to-spend-federal-aid-for-disaster-protection/*

Langford, T., & Keemahill, D. (2025, July 10). *Why Kerr County balked on a new flood warning system*. The Texas Tribune. *https://www.texastribune.org/2025/07/10/texas-kerr-county-commissioners-flooding-warning/#:~:text=In%202021%2C%20Kerr%20County%20was,%2C%E2%80%9D%20another%20resident%20told%20commissioners*

Wolman, J., Fertig, N., & Wolman, J. (2025, April 23). *Forest Service cuts leave states scrambling to prepare for summer wildfire season*. Politico. *https://www.politico.com/news/2025/04/23/crazy-forest-service-cuts-ignite-fear-fury-over-wildfire-risks-00301499*

Total Wildland Fires and Acres (1983-2024). (n.d.). National Interagency Fire Center. https://www.nifc.gov/fire-information/statistics/wildfires

FEMA. (n.d.). *Wildfire | National Risk Index*. Mapping Information Platform. *https://hazards.fema.gov/nri/wildfire*

Roebuck, S. (2025, May 22). *FEMA to resume in-person training at National Fire Academy*. FireRescue1. *https://www.firerescue1.com/national-fire-academy/fema-to-resume-in-person-training-at-national-fire-academy*

NIOSH Layoffs Hit Fire Service Programs Hard. (2025, April 3). Firefighter Nation. *https://www.firefighternation.com/health-wellness/physical-health/niosh-layoffs-fire-service-programs/*

Stearnbourne, C. (2025, May 20). *What's lost with NIOSH cuts: Q&A with David Christiani*. Harvard T.H. Chan School of Public Health. *https://hsph.harvard.edu/news/whats-lost-with-niosh-cuts-qa-with-david-christiani/*

Safety + Health. (2025, June 2). *The Chemical Safety Board faces elimination in White House FY 2026 budget proposal.* Safety+Health. https://www.safetyandhealthmagazine.com/articles/26901-the-chemical-safety-board-faces-elimination-in-white-house-fy-2026-budget-proposal

Safety + Health. (2025, September 10). *More details emerge on House appropriations bill for OSHA, MSHA, and NIOSH.* Safety+Health. https://www.safetyandhealthmagazine.com/articles/27286-more-details-emerge-on-house-appropriations-bill-for-osha-msha-and-niosh

Frazin, R. (2025, March 28) *DHS considers axing disaster and counterterrorism grants that help sanctuary cities.* The Hill. https://thehill.com/policy/energy-environment/5220804-dhs-considers-axing-disaster-and-counterterrorism-grants-that-help-sanctuary-cities/

State of California Department of Justice. (2025, May 13). *Attorney General Bonta Sues U.S. Departments of Transportation and Homeland Security Over Illegal Immigration Enforcement Conditions on Grant Funding.* California Department of Justice. *https://oag.ca.gov/news/press-releases/attorney-general-bonta-sues-us-departments-transportation-and-homeland-security*

Rosen, C. (2025, May 16). *Chicago sues Department of Homeland Security over counterterrorism program cuts.* Courthouse News Service. https://www.courthousenews.com/chicago-sues-department-of-homeland-security-over-counterterrorism-program-cuts/

Martin, H., Tomasko, L., Boris, E. T., Lecy, J., Faulk, L., & Kim, M. (2024, October 16). *Nonprofit trends and impacts 2021–2023: National findings on government grants and contracts from 2019 to 2023.* Urban Institute. https://www.urban.org/research/publication/nonprofit-trends-and-impacts-2021-2023-national-findings-government-grants-contracts-2019-2023

Clerkin, C., Koob, A., & Wolcheck, D. (2025, February 6). *How reliant are nonprofits on government grants?* Candid. https://candid.org/blogs/how-many-nonprofits-rely-on-government-grants-data/

Tomasko, L. (2025, February 21). *Government Funding Cuts Put Nonprofits at Risk across the Nation*. Urban Institute. *https://www.urban.org/urban-wire/government-funding-cuts-put-nonprofits-risk-across-nation*

Urban Institute (2025, September 5). *What is the Financial Risk of Non-Profits Losing Government Grants?* Data Visualization. Urban Institute. *https://www.urban.org/research/publication/what-financial-risk-nonprofits-losing-government-grants*

The White House. (2025, August 7). *Improving Oversight of Federal Grantmaking*. The White House. *https://www.whitehouse.gov/presidential-actions/2025/08/improving-oversight-of-federal-grantmaking/*

US Department of Health and Human Services (2025) *Fiscal Year 2026 Budget in Brief*. HHS.gov. *Fiscal Year 2026 Budget in Brief.*

Walker, J. (2025, October 3). FBI axes partnership with civil rights watchdog SPLC. *Axios*. https://www.axios.com/2025/10/03/fbi-ends-partnership-splc-civil-rights

CHAPTER 7: YOUR WORK

Goldberg, B., Sasfai, B., & Hooper, R. (2025, March 3). The changing tides of the SEC under the second Trump administration. Harvard Law School Forum on Corporate Governance. https://corpgov.law.harvard.edu/2025/03/03/the-changing-tides-of-the-sec-under-the-second-trump-administration/

Bonavitacola, J. (2025, May 13). Trump administration walks back mental health parity in insurance coverage. *The American Journal of Managed Care*. https://www.ajmc.com/view/trump-administration-walks-back-mental-health-parity-in-insurance-coverage

Coalition for a Democratic Workplace, Letter to Attorney General Pam Bondi Regarding Executive Order No. 14215 and NLRB Precedent (Apr. 3, 2025), https://myprivateballot.com/wp-content/uploads/2025/04/CDW-letter-to-AG-Bondi_EO-14215_Apr-2025.pdf.

McFerran, L., & Rhinehart, L. (2025, April 14). A coalition of hundreds of employers is asking the Trump administration to override the NLRB and dictate labor law. *Working Economics Blog*. Economic Policy Institute. https://www.epi.org/blog/a-coalition-of-hundreds-of-employers-is-asking-the-trump-administration-to-override-the-nlrb-and-dictate-labor-law/

Plunkett, J. J., Kelly, T. S., & Zagger, Z. V. (2025, July 18). Senate HELP Committee questions Trump nominees for EEOC commissioner, NLRB general counsel roles. *The National Law Review*. https://natlawreview.com/article/senate-help-committee-questions-trump-nominees-eeoc-commissioner-nlrb-general

Purifoy, P. (2025, March 31). *NLRB top cop pick primed to dismantle Biden-era legal precedents*. Bloomberg Law. https://news.bloomberglaw.com/daily-labor-report/nlrb-top-cop-pick-primed-to-dismantle-biden-era-legal-precedents

Markey, E. J., Cantwell, M., Shaheen, J., Booker, C. A., Coons, C. A., Hirono, M. K., Rosen, J., Hickenlooper, J., & Schiff, A. B. (2025, May 16). *Letter to Administrator Kelly Loeffler regarding SBA entrepreneurial development programs* [Letter]. U.S. Senate Committee on Small Business and Entrepreneurship. https://www.sbc.senate.gov/public/_cache/files/6/e/6e9679f2-a122-40c0-8e29-db71f04b69c8/83B6288B60A2529B17E362419E7ABCD-DD318B67E2E480460E45A660F97766ECA.ed-letter-to-sba-may-16-.pdf

U.S. Department of Labor. (2025). *FY 2026 Department of Labor budget in brief*. https://www.dol.gov/sites/dolgov/files/general/budget/2026/FY2026BIB.pdf

Johnson, D. (2025, May 30). White House opens OSHA budget battle. *Industrial Safety & Hygiene News*. https://www.ishn.com/articles/114767-white-house-opens-osha-budget-battle

Heckman, J. (2026, January 14). HHS reinstates all laid-off employees at workplace safety agency NIOSH. Federal News Network. https://federalnewsnetwork.com/workforce/2026/01/hhs-reinstates-all-laid-off-employees-at-workplace-safety-agency-niosh/

Mulholland, P. (2025, April 24). *EBSA loses over 20% of staff from resignations*. Plan Sponsor Council of America. https://www.psca.org/news/psca-news/2025/4/ebsa-loses-over-20-of-staff-from-resignations/

Iafolla, R., & Purifoy, P. (2025, May 30). *NLRB plans to cut staffers, save money without mass layoffs*. Bloomberg Law. https://news.bloomberglaw.com/daily-labor-report/nlrb-plans-to-cut-staffers-save-money-without-mass-layoffs

Finstad, B., Sponsor, (2025). *Save SBA from Sanctuary Cities Act of 2025*, H.R.2931, 119th Congress. https://www.congress.gov/bill/119th-congress/house-bill/2931

Vought, R. T. (2025, May 2). *Fiscal year 2026 discretionary budget request* [Letter to Chair Collins]. Office of Management and Budget, Executive Office of the President. https://www.whitehouse.gov/wp-content/uploads/2025/05/Fiscal-Year-2026-Discretionary-Budget-Request.pdf

Heckman, J. (2025, March 21). *SBA to cut 43% of workforce, return to pre-pandemic staffing levels*. Federal News Network. https://federalnewsnetwork.com/workforce/2025/03/sba-to-cut-43-of-workforce-return-to-pre-pandemic-staffing-levels/

U.S. Department of Labor. (n.d.). FY 2026 budget. https://www.dol.gov/general/budget

Feldscher, K. (2025, April 24). *NIOSH cuts threaten worker health and safety, say experts*. Harvard T.H. Chan School of Public Health. https://hsph.harvard.edu/news/niosh-cuts-threaten-worker-health-and-safety-say-experts/

Occupational Safety and Health Administration. (n.d.). *Current enforcement summary*. U.S. Department of Labor.

U.S. Department of the Treasury. (2023, August 28). *FACT SHEET: Treasury Department Releases First-Of-Its-Kind Report on Benefits of Unions to the U.S. Economy* [Press release].

Tierney, A. (2025, June 4). *Number of union members in the United States from 2000 to 2024 (in millions)*. Statista.

The White House. (2025, March 20). Additional rescissions of harmful executive orders and actions. Federal Register. https://www.federalregister.gov/documents/2025/03/20/2025-04866/additional-rescissions-of-harmful-executive-orders-and-actions

Paycom. (2025, July 3). *Your 2025 guide to every state's minimum wage*. https://www.paycom.com/resources/blog/minimum-wage-rate-by-state/

Miller, T. M., & Yuengert, A. R. (2021, January 7). Who's the boss? U.S. DOL issues final rule on independent contractor status. Employment Law Insights. https://www.employmentlawinsights.com/2021/01/whos-the-boss-u-s-dol-issues-final-rule-on-independent-contractor-status/

Nurden, H. (2024, November 1). An ongoing mental health epidemic: The need for stronger mental health parity laws in the U.S. Labor and Employment Law Section, American Bar Association. https://www.americanbar.org/groups/labor_law/resources/committee-articles/2024/ongoing-mental-health-epidemic-need-stronger-parity-laws/#:~:text=IV.-,The%20Mental%20Health%20Parity%20and%20Addiction%20Equity%20Act%20of%202008,mental%20illness%20and/or%20addiction

Bonavitacola, J. (2025, May 13). Trump administration walks back mental health parity in insurance coverage. *The American Journal of Managed Care*. https://www.ajmc.com/view/trump-administration-walks-back-mental-health-parity-in-insurance-coverage

Needels, K., Hawthorne, A., Shea, M., Westall, J., Saunders, C., & Clarkwest, A. (2024). Unemployment Insurance (UI) administrative funding and costs: A literature review. *Chief Evaluation Office, U.S. Department of Labor.* https://www.dol.gov/resource-library/unemployment-insurance-ui-administrative-funding-and-costs-literature-review

Job Corps. (2024, August 14). *Connecting Potential With Opportunity: 60 Years of Job Corps*. U.S. Department of Labor.

Bussewitz, C. (2025, June 5). Judge and lawmakers question the Trump administration's plan to gut Job Corps centers. AP News. https://apnews.com/article/job-corps-centers-lawsuit-labor-department-a9acc1464ad180a066317fd086865464

U.S. Chamber of Commerce. (2024, May 20). Small business data center. https://www.uschamber.com/small-business/small-business-data-center

Pew Research Center. (2024, April 22). A look at small businesses in the U.S. Retrieved from https://www.pewresearch.org/short-reads/2024/04/22/a-look-at-small-businesses-in-the-us/

Wells Fargo & Company. (2024, January 9). *New report finds growth of women business owners outpaces the market*. https://newsroom.wf.-

com/news-releases/news-details/2024/New-Report-Finds-Growth-of-Women-Business-Owners-Outpaces-the-Market/

Federal Reserve Bank of New York. (2017, November 30). Inaugural report on women-owned small businesses depicts reasons for gender gap. *Federal Reserve Bank of New York.* https://www.newyorkfed.org/newsevents/news/regional_outreach/2017/an171130#:~:text=Among%20recent%20credit%20applicants%2C%20women,50%25

Tayne Law Group, P.C. (2025). Small business loan statistics: Is sexism prevalent? Tayne Law Group. https://attorney-newyork.com/business-loan-statistics/

U.S. Small Business Administration. (2025). FY 2026 Congressional budget justification: Fiscal year 2026 annual performance plan. https://www.sba.gov/sites/default/files/2025-06/FY%202026%20CBJ%20FINAL%202025.05.29.pdf

CHAPTER 8: YOUR HOBBIES

U.S. Department of the Interior. (2025, May). The Interior: Fiscal year 2026 budget in brief. https://www.doi.gov/sites/default/files/documents/2025-06/fy26bibentire-book508060125_0.pdf

National Parks Conservation Association. (2025, May 5). President Trump's proposed budget could decimate at least 350 national park sites. NPCA.

Heckman, J. (2025, March 31). Agency funding libraries and museums puts all employees on leave ahead of major cuts. Federal News Network.

The White House. (2025, May 2). Fiscal Year 2026 discretionary budget request. https://www.whitehouse.gov/wp-content/uploads/2025/05/Fiscal-Year-2026-Discretionary-Budget-Request.pdf

Brown, J., & Epstein, S. (2025, June 4). Local arts groups face budget gaps as NEA pulls grants. PBS NewsHour. https://www.pbs.org/newshour/show/local-arts-groups-face-budget-gaps-as-nea-pulls-grants

Carrigan, M., & Boucher, B. (2025, May 8). All the arts organizations impacted by NEA funding cuts. Artnet News. https://news.artnet.com/art-world/nea-funding-cuts-2640963

Blair, E. (2025, April 10). Where did U.S. humanities grants go? To projects from a baseball film to AI research. NPR. https://www.npr.org/2025/04/10/nx-s1-5352821/national-endowment-humanities-grants-funding-terminated

Frazin, R. (2025, June 9). Trump's cuts to National Park Service rankle Republicans. The Hill. https://thehill.com/policy/energy-environment/5337528-trump-proposed-cuts-national-park-service/

American Library Association. (2025, May 21). ALA welcomes IMLS staff return and select grant reinstatements, cautiously optimistic about national case. ALA. https://www.ala.org/news/2025/05/ala-welcomes-imls-staff-return-and-select-grant-reinstatements-cautiously

National Park Service. (2021, February 2). Great American Outdoors Act. U.S. Department of the Interior. https://www.nps.gov/subjects/legal/great-american-outdoors-act.htm

Land and Water Conservation Fund Coalition. (n.d.). Outdoor Recreation Legacy Partnership program. https://lwcfcoalition.org/orlp

U.S. Department of the Interior, Office of Inspector General. (2023). The U.S. Department of the Interior does not analyze effective royalty rates (Report No. 2021–CR–042) [PDF]. https://www.doioig.gov/sites/default/files/2021-migration/Final%20Inspection%20Report_EffectiveRoyaltyRates_Public.pdf

McConville, D., Lutz, M., & Rowland-Shea, J. (2025, September 22). The Trump administration's expansive push to sell out public lands to the highest bidder. Center for American Progress. https://www.americanprogress.org/article/the-trump-administrations-expansive-push-to-sell-out-public-lands-to-the-highest-bidder/

U.S. Department of the Interior. (2024, November 8). Interior Department announces $16.45 billion in fiscal year 2024 energy revenue. https://www.doi.gov/pressreleases/interior-department-announces-1645-billion-fiscal-year-2024-energy-revenue#:~:text=Since%201982%2C%20the%20Department%20has,on%20federal%20lands%20and%20waters

U.S. Department of the Interior. (2022). FY 2023 Land and Water Conservation Fund – Permanent Funding. https://www.doi.gov/sites/doi.gov/files/fy-2023-lwcf-funding-allocations-doi-508_0.pdf

American Hiking Society. (n.d.). The Land and Water Conservation Fund. American Hiking Society. Retrieved September 30, 2025.

Trust for Public Land. (n.d.). The Land and Water Conservation Fund — Past projects. Retrieved September 30, 2025, from https://lwcf.tplgis.org/mappast/

National Park Service. (2025, September 22). Outdoor Recreation Legacy Partnership Grants Program. U.S. Department of the Interior. https://www.nps.gov/subjects/lwcf/orlp.htm

Sierra Club. (2025, June 2). Sierra Club statement as Trump budget guts Land and Water Conservation Fund. Sierra Club. https://www.sierraclub.org/press-releases/2025/06/sierra-club-statement-trump-budget-guts-land-and-water-conservation-fund#:~:text=WASHING-TON%2C%20DC%20%E2%80%93%20The%20Trump%20admin-istration's,term%2C%20permanently%20funded%20the%20LWCF

Frazin, R. (2025, June 12). Senate Republicans eye public land sales in 'big, beautiful bill'. The Hill. https://thehill.com/policy/energy-environment/5346383-senate-proposes-sale-2-million-acres/

Haggerty, M., & Rowland-Shea, J. (2025, February 20). Trump quietly plans to liquidate public lands to finance his sovereign wealth fund. Center for American Progress. https://www.american-progress.org/article/trump-quietly-plans-to-liquidate-public-lands-to-finance-his-sovereign-wealth-fund/

Gorge Friends. (2025, June). Footnote [Image]. https://gorge-friends.org/wp-content/uploads/2025/06/Footnote.png

National Park Service. (2024, September 10). Visitor spending effects — Economic contributions of National Park visitor spending. U.S. Department of the Interior. https://www.nps.gov/subjects/so-cialscience/vse.htm

American Alliance of Museums. (2025, February). Issue: National Endowment for the Arts. https://www.aam-us.org/pro-grams/advocacy/policy-issues/issue-national-endowment-for-the-arts/

Institute of Museum and Library Services. (n.d.). State allotment data. https://www.imls.gov/find-funding/funding-opportuni-ties/grants-to-states/state-allotment-data

National Endowment for the Humanities. (n.d.). Impact in states & jurisdictions. https://www.neh.gov/impact/states

Connecticut Library Association. (2025, April 10). IMLS Advocacy - 2025. https://ctlibraryassociation.org/IMLS-2025#:~:text=IMLS%20funds%20are%20used%20to,state%20library%20employees%2C%20at%20risk

Institute of Museum and Library Services. (n.d.). Grants to States: State profiles. https://www.imls.gov/grants/grants-state/state-profiles

CHAPTER 9: YOUR UTILITIES

Bittle, J., & Egan McCarthy, R. (2026, February 27). The Colorado River is nearing collapse. It's Trump's problem now. Grist. https://grist.org/politics/colorado-river-deal-trump-burgum/

Swanson, C. (2026, February 17). A deal still hasn't been reached between Lower Basin and Upper Basin states on management of Colorado River. CBS News Colorado. https://www.cbsnews.com/colorado/news/lower-basin-rejects-colorado-river-agreement-upper-basin-consensus/

U.S. Environmental Protection Agency. (2024, December). Water affordability needs assessment: Report to Congress (EPA 830-R-24-015) [PDF]. https://www.epa.gov/system/files/documents/2024-12/water-affordability-needs-assessment.pdf

Environmental Working Group. (2025, August 14). PFAS contamination in the U.S. Retrieved from https://www.ewg.org/interactive-maps/pfas_contamination/

Adams, Q. H., Chan, E. M. G., Spangler, K. R., Weinberger, K. R., Lane, K. J., Errett, N. A., Hess, J. J., Sun, Y., Wellenius, G. A., & Nori-Sarma, A. (2023). Examining the optimal placement of cooling centers to serve populations at high risk of extreme heat exposure in 81 US cities. Public Health Reports, 138(6), 955–962. https://doi.org/10.1177/00333549221148174 https://pubmed.ncbi.nlm.nih.gov/36726308/

Cloudscene. (n.d.). Data centers in United States — All. Retrieved September 30, 2025, from https://cloudscene.com/market/data-centers-in-united-states/all

PivIT Global. (2025). Data center energy consumption: Trends and environmental impact. PivIT Global. https://info.pivitglobal.com/blog/data-center-energy-consumption-environmental-impact#:~:text=Data%20centers%20are%20the%20backbone,homes%20for%20an%20entire%20year

U.S. Department of Energy. (2024, December 20). DOE releases new report evaluating increase in electricity demand from data centers. Energy.gov. https://www.energy.gov/articles/doe-releases-new-report-evaluating-increase-electricity-demand-data-centers

Sadasivam, N., & Aldern, C. (n.d.). What's behind your eye-popping power bill? We broke it down, region by region. Grist. https://grist.org/energy/power-bills-electricity-prices-state-by-state/#:~:text=It's%20no%20secret%20that%20U.S.,on%20reining%20in%20utility%20bills.

Federal Reserve Bank of Atlanta. (2023, August 10). Baseline for work: 92 percent of jobs require digital skills. Partners Update. https://www.atlantafed.org/community-development/publications/partners-update/2023/08/10/baseline-for-work-92-percent-of-jobs-require-digital-skills#:~:text=The%20analysis%20revealed%20that%2092,(see%20the%20figure%20below)

Peterson, D. M. (2024, July 23). U.S. commercial real estate is headed toward a crisis. Harvard Business Review. https://hbr.org/2024/07/u-s-commercial-real-estate-is-headed-toward-a-crisis

Federal Communications Commission. (2024). Statement of Chairwoman Jessica Rosenworcel: Inquiry concerning the deployment of advanced telecommunications capability to all

Americans in a reasonable and timely fashion, GN Docket No. 22-270, 2024 Section 706 Report (FCC 24-27). https://docs.fcc.gov/public/attachments/FCC-24-27A2.pdf

McBride, J., & Berman, N. (2024, May 2). How U.S. water infrastructure works. Council on Foreign Relations. https://www.cfr.org/backgrounder/how-us-water-infrastructure-works

Kwong, E., Huang, P., Carlson, R., & Ramirez, R. (2024, April 26). 10 years after Flint, the fight to replace lead pipes across the U.S. continues. NPR. https://www.npr.org/2024/04/26/1198909905/flint-water-lead-poisoning-anniversary-chicago

The White House. (2024, October 8). FACT SHEET: Biden-Harris administration issues final rule to replace lead pipes within a decade, announces new funding to deliver clean drinking water. https://bidenwhitehouse.archives.gov/press-releases/2024/10/08/fact-sheet-biden-harris-administration-issues-final-rule-replace-lead-pipes-within-decade/

U.S. Environmental Protection Agency. (2025, May 14). EPA announces it will keep maximum contaminant levels for PFOA, PFOS. EPA. https://www.epa.gov/newsreleases/epa-announces-it-will-keep-maximum-contaminant-levels-pfoa-pfos

Singer, A., & Kane, J. W. (2025, February 27). Millions of Americans lack affordable water access. Here's how local utilities can help. Brookings Institution. https://www.brookings.edu/articles/millions-of-americans-lack-affordable-water-access-heres-how-local-utilities-can-help/

Murray, P. (2025, June 11). Senator Murray opening remarks at hearing on Army Corps, Bureau of Reclamation budgets. Office of Senator Patty Murray. https://www.murray.senate.gov/senator-murray-opening-remarks-at-hearing-on-army-corps-bureau-of-reclamation-budgets/

Padilla, A. (2025, January 31). Padilla demands answers from Trump administration after Army Corps orders Central Valley dams open to dangerous flood levels. U.S. Senator Alex Padilla. https://www.padilla.senate.gov/newsroom/press-releases/padilla-demands-answers-from-trump-administration-after-army-corps-orders-central-valley-dams-open-to-dangerous-flood-levels/#:~:text=WASHINGTON%2C%20D.C.%20%E2%80%94%20Today%2C%20U.S

The White House. (2025, May 2). Fiscal Year 2026 discretionary budget request. Executive Office of the President, Office of Management and Budget. https://www.whitehouse.gov/wp-content/uploads/2025/05/Fiscal-Year-2026-Discretionary-Budget-Request.pdf

Jenkins, J. D., Farbes, J., Jones, R., Cheng, A., Luo, Q., & Haley, B. (2025). A Fork In The Road: Impacts of Federal Policy Repeal On The U.S. Energy Transition (Version v5) [Report]. REPEAT Project. https://zenodo.org/records/15497751

Chesapeake Climate Action Network Action Fund. (2025). House GOP's reconciliation bill cuts clean energy tax incentives, threatening hundreds of thousands of jobs and raising energy costs nationwide. https://ccanactionfund.org/house-gops-reconciliation-bill-cuts-clean-energy-tax-incentives-threatening-hundreds-of-thousands-of-jobs-and-raising-energy-costs-nationwide/

United States Senate Committee on Finance. (2025). Finance Committee legislative text: Title VII—Finance. https://www.finance.senate.gov/imo/media/doc/finance_committee_legislative_text_title_vii.pdf

The White House. (2025, January 20). Unleashing American energy. https://www.whitehouse.gov/presidential-actions/2025/01/unleashing-american-energy/

Lea, J. (2025, May 7). The Trump administration has attempted to cancel $23.3 billion in clean energy grants. Climate Program Portal. https://climateprogramportal.org/2025/05/07/the-trump-administration-has-attempted-to-cancel-23-3-billion-in-clean-energy-grants/

National Sustainable Agriculture Coalition. (2025, April 3). USDA begins releasing frozen REAP funding. NSAC's Blog. https://sustainableagriculture.net/blog/usda-begins-releasing-frozen-reap-funding/

Administration for Children and Families, Office of Community Services. (2024). LIHEAP fact sheet. U.S. Department of Health & Human Services. https://acf.gov/ocs/fact-sheet/liheap-fact-sheet

National Energy Assistance Directors' Association. (n.d.). *LIHEAP still here, but threats loom*. https://neada.org/press/liheap-under-threat/

Bergh, K., Rosenbaum, D., & Tharpe, W. (2025, May 28). House reconciliation bill proposes deepest SNAP cut in history, would take food assistance away from millions of low-income families. Center on Budget and Policy Priorities. https://www.cbpp.org/research/food-assistance/house-reconciliation-bill-proposes-deepest-snap-cut-in-history-would-take

House Committee on Agriculture. (2025). Reconciliation overview one-pager. U.S. House of Representatives. https://agriculture.house.gov/uploadedfiles/reconcilation_overview_one_pager.pdf

Waldman, M. (2025, June 17). The budget bill's troubling AI provision. Brennan Center for Justice. https://www.brennancenter.org/our-work/analysis-opinion/budget-bills-troubling-ai-provision

Shahi, M. (2025, June 12). The Senate Republican budget bill adds broadband funding that favors Musk's Starlink and bans state AI laws. Center for American Progress. https://www.americanprogress.org/article/the-senate-republican-budget-bill-adds-broadband-funding-that-favors-musks-starlink-and-bans-state-ai-laws/

U.S. Senate Committee on Commerce, Science, and Transportation. (2024). Coast Guard Mission Readiness; Spectrum Auctions; Air Traffic Control Improvements; Space Launch and Reentry Licensing and Permitting; Mars, Artemis, Moon to Mars Program [Legislative text]. https://www.commerce.senate.gov/services/files/AD3D04CF-52B4-411F-854B-44C55ABBADDA

Weil, G. (2025, May 30). The House reconciliation bill's AI preemption clearly violates the Byrd Rule. Lawfare. https://www.lawfaremedia.org/article/the-house-reconciliation-bill-s-ai-preemption-clearly-violates-the-byrd-rule

Khatib, M. (2025, May 21). Big EV cuts proposed in federal budget text – here's what to know. EV Hub. https://www.atlasevhub.com/weekly-digest/big-ev-cuts-proposed-in-federal-budget-text-heres-what-to-know/#:~:text=This%20follows%20the%20Trump%20administration's,Atlas%20public%20brief%20or%20digest

Clean Economy Tracker. (n.d.). Atlas Public Policy & Utah State University. Retrieved September 30, 2025, from https://cleaneconomytracker.org/

Laing, K. (2025, February 7). Trump halts program to expand EV charger network. Transport Topics. https://www.ttnews.com/articles/trump-halts-ev-charger

U.S. Environmental Protection Agency. (2025). Greenhouse Gas Reduction Fund. EPA. https://www.epa.gov/aboutepa/greenhouse-gas-reduction-fund#:~:text=EPA%20Awards%20%2427%20Billion%20in,national%20nonprofit%20clean%20financing%20institutions

U.S. Department of Agriculture, Rural Development. (n.d.). Rural Energy for America Program (REAP).

Clayton, C. (2025, March 26). USDA reinstates rural energy funding but projects must align with Trump energy mandate. DTN Progressive Farmer. https://www.dtnpf.com/agriculture/web/ag/news/article/2025/03/26/usda-reinstates-rural-energy-funding

Khatib, M. (2025, May 21). Big EV cuts proposed in federal budget text – here's what to know. EV Hub. https://www.atlasevhub.com/weekly-digest/big-ev-cuts-proposed-in-federal-budget-text-heres-what-to-know/#:~:text=This%20follows%20the%20Trump%20administration's,Atlas%20public%20brief%20or%20digest

CHAPTER 10: YOUR FAMILY

Legal Services Corporation. (2025). Section 2: Today's low-income America. The Justice Gap Report. Retrieved September 30, 2025, from https://justicegap.lsc.gov/resource/section-2-todays-low-income-america/

Centers for Medicare & Medicaid Services. (2024, May). 2024 Medicaid & CHIP beneficiaries at a glance: Maternal health. U.S. Department of Health and Human Services. https://www.medicaid.gov/medicaid/benefits/downloads/2024-maternal-health-at-a-glance.pdf

Kayser, A. (2025, April 16). Maternity hospitals fear a Medicaid squeeze. Newsweek. https://www.newsweek.com/maternity-hospitals-fear-medicaid-squeeze-2060679

Kaiser Family Foundation. (2025, July 30). A closer look at the work requirement provisions in the 2025 federal budget reconciliation law. KFF. https://www.kff.org/medicaid/a-closer-look-at-the-work-requirement-provisions-in-the-2025-federal-budget-reconciliation-law/

Burns, A., & Rudowitz, R. (2025, June 18). Which states might have to reduce provider taxes under the Senate reconciliation bill? KFF.

Kaiser Family Foundation. (2025, February 13). Eliminating the Medicaid expansion federal match rate: State-by-state estimates. KFF.

Center for Healthcare Quality and Payment Reform. (2017). Rural hospitals at risk of closing [PDF]. https://web.archive.org/web/20250508125546/https:/chqpr.org/downloads/Rural_Hospitals_at_Risk_of_Closing.pdf

American Hospital Association. (2025, June 13). Rural hospitals at risk: Cuts to Medicaid would further threaten access. https://www.aha.org/fact-sheets/2025-06-13-rural-hospitals-risk-cuts-medicaid-would-further-threaten-access

Centers for Disease Control and Prevention, National Center for Health Statistics. (2025, August 20). Fertility rate: Live births per 1,000 women ages 15–44. https://www.cdc.gov/nchs/state-stats/births/fertility-rate.html?CDC_AAref_Val=https://www.cdc.gov/nchs/pressroom/sosmap/fertility_rate/fertility_rates.htm

March of Dimes. (2024). Nowhere to go: Maternity care deserts across the US. https://www.marchofdimes.org/maternity-care-deserts-report

Malde, J. (2025, April 28). What's on the table? A review of federal paid family leave proposals. Bipartisan Policy Center. https://bipartisanpolicy.org/explainer/whats-on-the-table-a-review-of-federal-paid-family-leave-proposals/

House Committee on Rules. (2025). Amendment to rules committee: Enhancement of paid family and medical leave credit (Print 119–3) [PDF]. https://amendments-rules.house.gov/amendments/Paid%20Leave%2045S%20Amdt250520132834986.pdf

Malde, J. (2025, April 30). What's in the bills: The More Paid Leave for More Americans Act and Interstate Paid Leave Action Network Act. Bipartisan Policy Center. https://bipartisanpolicy.org/blog/whats-in-the-bills-the-more-paid-leave-for-more-americans-act-and-interstate-paid-leave-action-network-act/

U.S. Congress. H.R. 3089, More Paid Leave for More Americans Act, 119th Cong., 1st sess. (2025). PDF. https://www.congress.gov/119/bills/hr3089/BILLS-119hr3089ih.pdf

Williamson, M. W. (2025, January 15). The state of paid family and medical leave in the U.S. in 2025. Center for American Progress. https://www.americanprogress.org/article/the-state-of-paid-family-and-medical-leave-in-the-u-s-in-2025/#:~:text=However%2C%20as%20of%202023%2C%20Bureau,access%20to%20paid%20family%20leave

U.S. Department of Health and Human Services, Administration for Children, Families, and Communities. (2025). FY 2026 Justification of Estimates Appropriations Committees. HHS. https://www.hhs.gov/sites/default/files/fy-2026-acfc-cj.pdf

Murray, P. (2025, April 16). NEW: Trump admin withholding nearly $1 billion in funding for Head Start—crunching centers nationwide and forcing devastating closures. Office of U.S. Senator Patty Murray. https://www.murray.senate.gov/new-trump-admin-withholding-nearly-1-billion-in-funding-for-head-start-crunching-centers-nationwide-and-forcing-devastating-closures/

Senate Committee on Appropriations. (2025, April 24). Letter to the Honorable Robert F. Kennedy, Jr., Secretary, U.S. Department of Health and Human Services: Re: actions undermining Head Start

[PDF]. https://www.appropriations.senate.gov/imo/media/doc/letter_on_hhs_attacks_on_head_start.pdf

First Five Years Fund. (2025, June 17). Overview: White House budget request, FY2026. First Five Years Fund.

First Five Years Fund. (2024, November). 2024: ABCs of federal early learning and child care funding streams. First Five Years Fund. https://www.ffyf.org/resources/2024/11/abcs-of-federal-early-learning-and-child-care-funding-streams-2024/

First Five Years Fund. (2025, January 31). Total federal TANF & state MOE expenditures for child care and early learning in FY 2023. First Five Years Fund.

U.S. House Committee on Ways and Means. (2024). Ways and Means Committee: Policy options and estimates [PDF]. Politico. https://www.politico.com/f/?id=00000194-74a8-d40a-ab9e-7fbc70940000

Child Care Aware® of America. (2025, May). Child care in America: 2024 price & supply. https://www.childcareaware.org/price-landscape24/

Center for the Study of Child Care Employment. (2024). Early childhood workforce index 2024: Executive summary—Key findings. UC Berkeley. https://cscce.berkeley.edu/workforce-index-2024/executive-summary/key-findings/

Center on Budget and Policy Priorities. (2025, June 27). Tracking Senate action on tax and budget reconciliation plan. CBPP. https://www.cbpp.org/blog/tracking-senate-action-on-tax-and-budget-reconciliation-plan?entry_uuid=f293d5e0-287f-447d-9e71-a8ba89dd6f43#entry

Turner, C. (2025, June 20). What children in poverty could lose from the 'Big Beautiful Bill'. NPR. https://www.npr.org/2025/06/20/nx-s1-5437851/children-poverty-republicans-big-beautiful-bill-reconciliation

Internal Revenue Service. (2025, September 16). EITC fast facts. https://www.irs.gov/credits-deductions/individuals/earned-income-tax-credit/eitc-fast-facts

Leiserson, G. (2025, May 28). The GOP plan to cut the EITC via administrative burdens. The Tax Law Center at NYU Law. https://taxlawcenter.org/blog/the-gop-plan-to-cut-the-eitc-via-administrative-burdens#:~:text=The%20version%20of%20the%20reconciliation,Income%20Tax%20Credit%20(EITC)

CHAPTER 11: YOUR MONEY

Aspan, M. (2025, March 4). The FDIC's goal is to prevent another banking crisis. It's now also a Trump target. *Oregon Public Broadcasting*. https://www.opb.org/article/2025/03/04/why-the-job-cuts-at-bank-regulator-fdic-are-raising-alarms/

Seligman, J., Coates, J., Coffee, J. C., Jr., Cox, J. D., Fisch, J. E., & Fox, M. B. (2025, February 24). Shadow SEC: The value of an independent SEC. *The CLS Blue Sky Blog*. https://clsbluesky.law.columbia.edu/2025/02/24/the-shadow-sec-the-value-of-an-independent-sec/

Horsley, S. (2025, June 18). Social Security benefits face big cuts in 2033, unless Congress acts. *NPR*. https://www.npr.org/2025/06/18/nx-s1-5436828/social-security-benefits-cut-congress

Lee, J., & Wessel, D. (2024, January 25). What did the Fed do after Silicon Valley Bank and Signature Bank failed? *Brookings Institution*. https://www.brookings.edu/articles/what-did-the-fed-do-after-silicon-valley-bank-and-signature-bank-failed/

Turner, J. (2023, March 17). Why did Silicon Valley Bank fail? *Economics Observatory*. https://www.economicsobservatory.com/why-did-silicon-valley-bank-fail

Cipriani, M., Eisenbach, T. M., & Kovner, A. (2024, December). Anatomy of the bank runs in March 2023. *Economic Brief*, No. 24-39. Federal Reserve Bank of Richmond. https://www.richmondfed.org/publications/research/economic_brief/2024/eb_24-39#:~:text=In%20other%20words%2C%20the%20March,mainly%20initiated%20by%20larger%20depositors

Board of Governors of the Federal Reserve System. (2023, April). *Review of the Federal Reserve's supervision and regulation of Silicon Valley Bank*. https://www.federalreserve.gov/publications/files/svb-review-20230428.pdf

U.S. Equal Employment Opportunity Commission. (n.d.). Federal Deposit Insurance Corporation (FDIC). https://www.eeoc.gov/federal-sector/federal-deposit-insurance-corporation-fdic-0#:~:text=Permanent%20Workforce:%205%2C280%20Temporary%20Workforce:%202%2C869%20Total%20Workforce:%208%2C149

Saulsbery, G. (2025, April 22). FDIC aims to reduce workforce by 1,250. *Banking Dive*. https://www.bankingdive.com/news/fdic-aims-reduce-workforce-1250/746020/#:~:text=The%20Federal%20Deposit%20Insurance%20Corp,%2C%E2%80%9D%20according%20to%20the%20memo

Petry, E., & Vandewalker, I. (2025, February 24). Who benefits from Trump's move to shut down Consumer Financial Protection Bureau? *Brennan Center for Justice*. https://www.brennancenter.org/our-work/analysis-opinion/who-benefits-trumps-move-shut-down-consumer-financial-protection-bureau

Schroeder, P. (2025, June 20). US Senate referee rules against cuts to CFPB, financial regulators in tax and spending bill. *Reuters*. https://www.reuters.com/legal/government/us-senate-referee-rules-against-cuts-cfpb-financial-regulators-tax-spending-bill-2025-06-20/

Reuters. (2025, June 23). Trump's CFPB rollback has cost Americans $18 billion, consumer groups say. *The Economic Times*. https://economictimes.indiatimes.com/news/international/global-trends/trumps-cfpb-rollback-has-cost-americans-18-billion-consumer-groups-say/articleshow/122045516.cms?from=mdr

Dayen, D. (2024, March 5). Congress poised to kneecap antitrust division. *The American Prospect*. https://prospect.org/politics/2024-03-05-congress-poised-kneecap-antitrust-division/

Weiner, M. L., & Carr, M. (2025, May 5). "America First Antitrust": New policy or new terminology? *StepAhead: Antitrust & Competition Insights*. Steptoe LLP. https://www.steptoe.com/en/news-publications/stepahead-antitrust-and-competition-insights/america-first-antitrust-new-policy-or-new-terminology.html

Sokler, B. D., Kidwell, R. G., & Thornton, P. T. (2025, May 6). Trump antitrust enforcers outline "America first" antitrust enforcement. *Mintz*. https://www.mintz.com/insights-center/viewpoints/2191/2025-05-06-trump-antitrust-enforcers-outline-america-first#_ftn12

Partington, R. (2025, April 8). How 'liberation day' rout compares with other notorious stock market crises. *The Guardian*. https://www.theguardian.com/business/2025/apr/08/how-liberation-day-rout-compares-with-other-notorious-stock-market-crises

Assis, C. (2025, June 5). Tesla has lost nearly $200 billion in market cap since Elon Musk left 'DOGE.' Here's what may be ahead for the stock. *MarketWatch*. https://www.marketwatch.com/story/tesla-has-lost-nearly-140-billion-in-market-cap-since-elon-musk-left-doge-heres-what-may-be-ahead-for-the-stock-4ad8257f

Butrica, B. A., Smith, K. E., & Toder, E. J. (2009). *What the 2008 stock market crash means for retirement security* (Discussion Paper 09-03). The Urban Institute. https://www.urban.org/sites/default/files/publication/30291/411876-What-the-Stock-Market-Crash-Means-for-Retirement-Security.PDF

U.S. Securities and Exchange Commission. (n.d.). The role of the SEC. Investor.gov. https://www.investor.gov/introduction-investing/investing-basics/role-sec#:~:text=Mission,Facilitate%20capital%20formation

U.S. Securities and Exchange Commission. (2025, August 13). Search filings. https://www.sec.gov/search-filings

U.S. Securities and Exchange Commission. (n.d.). Introduction to investing. Investor.gov. Retrieved October 1, 2025, from https://www.investor.gov/introduction-investing

Securities and Exchange Commission v. Jarkesy, No. 22–859 (U.S. June 27, 2024), slip op., https://www.supremecourt.gov/opinions/23pdf/22-859_1924.pdf

Associated Press. (2025, September 15). Trump says the US should do away with quarterly earnings reports. AP News. https://apnews.com/article/trump-quarterly-earnings-reports-sec-semiannual-cd5fbed69b72e7525848bc11109d0d35

Prentice, C., & Gillison, D. (2025, May 6). U.S. SEC's new chief says 15% of staff have left, contract cuts to come, sources say. Reuters. https://www.reuters.com/business/world-at-work/us-secs-new-chief-says-15-staff-have-left-contract-cuts-come-sources-say-

2025-05-06/#:~:text=WASHINGTON%2C%20-May%206%20(Reuters),sources%20familiar%20with%20the%20matter

Coates, J., Coffee, J. C., Jr., Cox, J. D., Fox, M. B., & Seligman, J. (2025, March 13). Shadow SEC Statement No. 2: The crisis deepens as SEC staff and budget cuts are directed. CLS Blue Sky: Columbia Law School Blog on Corporations and the Capital Markets. https://clsbluesky.law.columbia.edu/2025/03/13/shadow-sec-statement-no-2-march-13-2025-the-crisis-deepens-as-sec-staff-and-budget-cuts-are-directed/#:~:text=Beyond%20actually%20unlawful%20acts%20or,the%20timely%20responses%20they%20desire

The White House. (2025, January 20). Regulatory freeze pending review. https://www.whitehouse.gov/presidential-actions/2025/01/regulatory-freeze-pending-review/

The White House. (2025, February 6). Unleashing prosperity through deregulation (Exec. Order No. 14192). Federal Register. https://www.federalregister.gov/documents/2025/02/06/2025-02345/unleashing-prosperity-through-deregulation

Goldberg, B., Sasfai, B., & Hooper, R. (2025, March 3). The changing tides of the SEC under the second Trump administration. Harvard Law School Forum on Corporate Governance. https://corpgov.law.harvard.edu/2025/03/03/the-changing-tides-of-the-sec-under-the-second-trump-administration/

The White House. (2025, February 10). Pausing Foreign Corrupt Practices Act enforcement to further American economic and national security. https://www.whitehouse.gov/presidential-actions/2025/02/pausing-foreign-corrupt-practices-act-enforcement-to-further-american-economic-and-national-security/

Hill, J. F. (2025). H.R.3394 — Fair Investment Opportunities for Professional Experts Act. 119th Congress. Retrieved from https://www.congress.gov/bill/119th-congress/house-bill/3394

U.S. Securities and Exchange Commission. (2024, June 28). Exemption for limited offerings not exceeding $10 million — Rule 504 of Regulation D. https://www.sec.gov/resources-small-businesses/exempt-offerings/exemption-limited-offerings-not-exceeding-10-million-rule-504-regulation-d

U.S. Department of Labor. (2024). 29 C.F.R. § 2510.3-21 — Definition of "Fiduciary." Retrieved from https://www.law.cornell.edu/cfr/text/29/2510.3-21

Warren & Siurek, L.L.P. (2019, March 13). How Studebaker's failure inspired ERISA. Warren & Siurek, L.L.P. Blog. https://www.warrensiurek.com/blog/2019/03/how-studebakers-failure-inspired-erisa/

Pension Benefit Guaranty Corporation. (n.d.). History. U.S. Department of Labor. Retrieved October 1, 2025, from https://www.pbgc.gov/about/who-we-are/history#:~:text=In%201974%2C%20Congress%20passed%20the,needed%20to%20collect%20premium%20payments

Van Bramer, J. (2025, June 4). EBSA requests slimmer budget, fewer employees for 2026. PLANSPONSOR. https://www.plansponsor.com/ebsa-requests-slimmer-budget-fewer-employees-for-2026/

Godbout, T. (2025, June 6). Aronowitz pledges 'major turn-around' for EBSA if confirmed. ASPPA. https://www.asppanet.org/news/2025/6/aronowitz-pledges-major-turn-around-for-ebsa-if-confirmed/#:~:text=As%20to%20those%20three%20goals,cybersecurity%20to%20protect%20participant%20assets

Carosa, C. (2025, January 22). Most likely & immediate Trump changes to fiduciary & ERISA plans. Carington Financial — Your Caring Advisor. https://www.yourcaringadvisor.-

com/blog/most-likely-immediate-trump-changes-to-fiduciary-erisa-plans

Mattingly, P. (2025, July 16). Warren warns Trump's policies could lead to another economic crash. CNN. https://www.cnn.com/2025/07/16/politics/elizabeth-warren-trump-financial-crisis?iid=cnn_buildContentRecirc_end_recirc&recs_exp=up-next-article-end&tenant_id=related.en

The White House. (2025, August 7). Democratizing access to alternative assets for 401(k) investors. https://www.whitehouse.gov/presidential-actions/2025/08/democratizing-access-to-alternative-assets-for-401k-investors/

DeSilver, D. (2025, May 20). What the data says about Social Security. Pew Research Center. https://www.pewresearch.org/short-reads/2025/05/20/what-the-data-says-about-social-security/

The White House. (2025, March 11). FACT CHECK: President Trump will always protect Social Security, Medicare. https://www.whitehouse.gov/articles/2025/03/fact-check-president-trump-will-always-protect-social-security-medicare/

Markowitz, A. (2025, February 28). Social Security Administration plans 'significant' staff reductions. AARP. https://www.aarp.org/social-security/ssa-workforce-reductions/

Jassin, L. (2025, March 7). List of Social Security Administration offices DOGE is closing. NEWS10. https://www.news10.com/news/list-of-social-security-administration-offices-doge-is-closing/#:~:text=The%20latest%20announcement%20from%20DOGE,Jasper

Social Security Administration. (2025, March 27). Correcting the record about Social Security office closings. Social Security Matters. Last updated April 18, 2025.

Social Security Administration. (2025, March 18; last updated June 24, 2025). Social Security strengthens identity proofing requirements and expedites direct deposit changes to one day. Social Security Matters. https://blog.ssa.gov/social-security-strengthens-identity-proofing-requirements-and-expedites-direct-deposit-changes-to-one-day/

Markowitz, A. (2025, April 9). Social Security drops most restrictions on benefit claims by phone. AARP. https://www.aarp.org/social-security/planned-id-verification-requirements-eased.html

Pan, J. (2025, March 28). Howard Lutnick says his 94-year-old mother-in-law 'wouldn't complain' if Social Security missed a payment — claims 'real America' will be rewarded while the fraudsters 'yell and scream'. Yahoo Finance. https://finance.yahoo.com/news/howard-lutnick-says-mother-law-104500599.html?guccounter=1&guce_referrer=aHR0cHM6Ly9kb2NzLmdvb2dsZS5jb20v&guce_referrer_sig=AQAAALBd27uLrfcmTcJdfR0sNjaEvpra_BfeTgE6-66m-RoFVJ1qCMRheHtk70UjzYERGHrEA-v7n-YDM8l_Wj4H6N-RiogHf

Krugman, P. (2025, March 19). Smears, sadism and Social Security. Paul Krugman. https://paulkrugman.substack.com/p/smears-sadism-and-social-security

Hager, E. (2025, March 12). "The president wanted it and I did it": Recording reveals head of Social Security's thoughts on DOGE and Trump. ProPublica. https://www.propublica.org/article/recording-reveals-leland-dudek-thoughts-trump-doge-social-security

Center on Budget and Policy Priorities. (2025, April 23). Immigrants contribute greatly to the Social Security trust fund's solvency. CBPP. https://www.cbpp.org/blog/immigrants-contribute-greatly-to-the-social-security-trust-funds-solvency

Perez, D., & Morrissey, M. (2025, May 13). Southern and Midwestern districts are the most vulnerable to Social Security cuts and disruptions. *Economic Policy Institute.* https://www.epi.org/blog/southern-and-midwestern-districts-are-the-most-vulnerable-to-social-security-cuts-and-disruptions/

CHAPTER 12: YOUR ENVIRONMENT

Olival, K. J., Hoguet, R. L., & Daszak, P. (2013). Linking the historical roots of environmental conservation with human and wildlife health. EcoHealth, 10(3), 224–227. https://doi.org/10.1007/s10393-013-0862-2 https://pmc.ncbi.nlm.nih.gov/articles/PMC3914161/

Environmental History. (n.d.). The Sixties: 1960–1969. EnvironmentalHistory.org. https://environmentalhistory.org/20th-century/sixties-1960-1969/

Rothman, L. (2017, March 22). Here's why the Environmental Protection Agency was created. TIME. https://time.com/4696104/environmental-protection-agency-1970-history/

Cram, D. S., Ashcroft, N. K., Smallidge, S. T., & Owen, L. P. (2017). An introduction to NEPA: The National Environmental Policy Act of 1969 (RITF 85). College of Agriculture, Consumer and Environmental Sciences, New Mexico State University.

Tulane University Law School. (2021, June 15). History of the Clean Water Act. Tulane Online — Blog. https://online.law.tulane.edu/blog/clean-water-act-history

Weinmeyer, R., Norling, A., Kawarski, M., & Higgins, E. (2017, October). The Safe Drinking Water Act of 1974 and its role in providing access to safe drinking water in the United States. AMA Journal of Ethics. https://journalofethics.ama-assn.org/article/safe-drinking-water-act-1974-and-its-role-providing-access-safe-drinking-water-united-states/2017-10

Hu, S. (2025, August 11). The Clean Air Act 101. Natural Resources Defense Council. https://www.nrdc.org/stories/clean-air-act-101#climate

U.S. Environmental Protection Agency. (2025, February 14). Superfund's 40th anniversary — A look-back at the decades. https://www.epa.gov/superfund/superfunds-40th-anniversary-look-back-decades

U.S. Environmental Protection Agency, Office of Land and Emergency Management. (2023). Population surrounding 1,881 Superfund sites (FY2022 population estimates) [PDF]. https://www.epa.gov/system/files/documents/2023-08/FY22%20Population%20Estimates%20Superfund%20Final.pdf

U.S. Environmental Protection Agency. (2025, September 22). Superfund: CERCLA overview. https://www.epa.gov/superfund/superfund-cercla-overview

United States Environmental Protection Agency. (n.d.). Superfund National Priorities List (NPL) Where You Live Map [Web map]. ArcGIS Online. https://epa.maps.arcgis.com/apps/webappviewer/index.html?id=33cebcdfdd1b4c3a8b51d416956c41f1

McCarthy, G., & Burke, T. A. (2017). We need a strong Environmental Protection Agency: It's about public health! American Journal of Public Health, 107(5), 649–651. https://doi.org/10.2105/AJPH.2017.303728

https://pmc.ncbi.nlm.nih.gov/articles/PMC5388973/

U.S. Department of the Interior, Office of the Assistant Secretary for Policy, Management and Budget. (n.d.). Policy & environmental management. https://www.doi.gov/pmb/pem

Council on Environmental Quality. (n.d.). Guidance. U.S. Council on Environmental Quality. https://ceq.doe.gov/guidance/guidance.html

National Institutes of Health. (n.d.). National Environmental Policy Act. NIH Environmental Management System. Retrieved October 1, 2025.

National Oceanic and Atmospheric Administration. (2025, March 5). About our agency. U.S. Department of Commerce. https://www.noaa.gov/about-our-agency#:~:text=From%20daily%20weather%20forecasts%2C%20severe,Our%20mission

National Association of State Departments of Agriculture Research Foundation; National Center for Agricultural Law Research and Information; Natural Resources Conservation Service; U.S. Environmental Protection Agency. (2000). Federal environmental laws affecting agriculture [PDF]. https://efotg.sc.egov.usda.gov/references/public/NY/Federal.pdf

Denchak, M. (2023, January 11). Water pollution: Everything you need to know. NRDC. https://www.nrdc.org/stories/water-pollution-everything-you-need-know

U.S. Department of Transportation. (n.d.). Environment and permitting. https://www.transportation.gov/policy/transportation-policy/environment

U.S. Department of Housing and Urban Development, Office of Environment and Energy. (n.d.). Environmental review. HUD Exchange. Retrieved October 1, 2025, from https://www.hudexchange.info/programs/environmental-review/

U.S. Army Corps of Engineers. (n.d.). Environmental Program. U.S. Army Corps of Engineers. https://www.usace.army.mil/Missions/Environmental/

Engels, S. H., Mergen, A. C., & Pidot, J. (2025, February 4). Crisis at DOJ's Environment & Natural Resources Division. Legal Planet. https://legal-planet.org/2025/02/04/crisis-at-dojs-environment-natural-resources-division/

U.S. Department of Labor. (n.d.). Summary of the major laws of the Department of Labor. https://www.dol.gov/general/about-dol/majorlaws

U.S. Department of Commerce. (2022, June 30). U.S. Department of Commerce climate adaptation plan: 2022 progress report. https://www.sustainability.gov/pdfs/doc-2022-cap.pdf

U.S. Department of Energy. (2025, May 12). Energy Department slashes 47 burdensome and costly regulations, delivering first milestone in America's biggest deregulatory effort. Energy.gov. https://www.energy.gov/articles/energy-department-slashes-47-burdensome-and-costly-regulations-delivering-first-milestone

Centers for Disease Control and Prevention. (n.d.). National Center for Environmental Health. U.S. Department of Health and Human Services. Retrieved October 1, 2025, from https://www.cdc.gov/nceh/index.html

Sabin Center for Climate Change Law. (n.d.). Climate Backtracker. Columbia Law School. Retrieved October 1, 2025, from https://climate.law.columbia.edu/content/climate-backtracker

Koshmrl, M. (2025, April 14). Trump's ag boss declares 113M-acre logging 'emergency.' Will it keep Wyoming's timber industry alive? WyoFile. https://wyofile.com/trumps-ag-boss-declares-113m-acre-logging-emergency-will-it-keep-wyomings-timber-industry-alive/

Sussman, M. S., Lafferty, S. G., Bunger, B. C., Lieban, E. M., Pilchen, Z., Holtan, A. S., Kriha, A., & Edwards, A. L. (2025, May 14). An update on climate superfund laws and climate change lawsuits. Holland & Knight. https://www.hklaw.com/en/insights/publications/2025/05/an-update-on-climate-superfund-laws-and-climate-change-lawsuits

U.S. Environmental Protection Agency. (2025, March 12). EPA launches biggest deregulatory action in U.S. history. https://www.epa.gov/newsreleases/epa-launches-biggest-deregulatory-action-us-history?fbclid=IwY2xjawLLkdlleHRu-A2FlbQIxMABicmlkETFaOWlCVDQyZDdlb21jM2tSAR7WUKB-wHFUA46nZnx84yv0_xljTswx7aIR1-0DSTu1ydqTOn9GrEemDiry3wA_aem_VI2D3mAPuAuzIDf-pkX8YAg

U.S. Department of Justice, Environment and Natural Resources Division. (n.d.). Retrieved [insert retrieval date], from https://www.justice.gov/enrd

U.S. Department of the Interior. (2025, April 23). Department of the Interior implements emergency permitting procedures to strengthen domestic energy supply. https://www.doi.gov/press-releases/department-interior-implements-emergency-permitting-procedures-strengthen-domestic

Frazin, R. (2025, June 25). Revised GOP plan would sell up to 1.2M acres of public lands. The Hill. https://thehill.com/policy/energy-environment/5369309-mike-lee-gop-budget-plan-public-lands-sale-trump-blm-national-forests/

Lawyers for Good Government. (2025, June 25). L4GG brings suit on behalf of nonprofits, Tribes and local governments with terminated EPA grants. Lawyers for Good Government. https://www.lawyersforgoodgovernment.org/blog/2025/6/25/l4gg-brings-suit-on-behalf-of-nonprofits-tribes-and-local-governments-with-terminated-epa-grants#:~:text=Washington%2C%20D.C.%20%E2%80%94Today%2C%20a,Congressional%20directive%20to%20fund%20them

Holland & Knight. (2025, June 5). EPA proposes significant budget reduction for fiscal year 2026. Holland & Knight. https://www.hklaw.com/en/insights/publications/2025/06/epa-proposes-significant-budget-reduction-for-fiscal-year-2026#:~:text=The%20U.S.%20Environmental%20Protection%20Agency's,regulatory%20actions%20to%20be%20pursued

Wallace, J. (2025, June 5). Trump's EPA budget would cut funds appropriated for waste offices. Waste Dive. https://www.wastedive.com/news/trumps-epa-budget-would-cut-funds-appropriated-for-waste-offices/749943/

United States Environmental Protection Agency. (2025). FY 2026 EPA budget in brief (Publication No. EPA-190-R-25-001) [PDF]. https://www.epa.gov/system/files/documents/2025-05/fy-2026-epa-bib.pdf

van Deelen, G. (2025, April 29). EPA to cancel nearly 800 environmental justice grants. Eos. https://eos.org/research-and-developments/epa-to-cancel-nearly-800-environmental-justice-grants

U.S. Environmental Protection Agency. (2026, January 21). Updated definition of waters of the United States. https://www.epa.gov/wotus/updated-definition-waters-united-states

Environmental Defense Fund. (2025, November 17). Trump proposal will dismantle wetlands protections, increase flood risk [Press release]. https://www.edf.org/media/trump-proposal-will-dismantle-wetlands-protections-increase-flood-risk

Environmental Defense Fund. (2025). Trump EPA pollution pass map. Retrieved October 1, 2025, from https://www.edf.org/maps/epa-pollution-pass/

Newsom, G. (2025, June 12). 'Assault on California continues': Governor Newsom sues Trump over illegal attempt to revoke state's clean air policies. Office of the Governor — State of California. https://www.gov.ca.gov/2025/06/12/assault-on-california-continues-governor-newsom-sues-trump-over-illegal-attempt-to-revoke-states-clean-air-policies/

Dieckman, E. (2025, March 27). Survey from Trump administration asks researchers abroad about involvement in DEI, environmental justice, and climate projects. Eos. https://eos.org/research-and-developments/survey-from-trump-administration-asks-researchers-abroad-about-involvement-in-dei-environmental-justice-and-climate-projects

National Science Foundation. (2025, April 18). Updates on NSF priorities — Why is NSF terminating awards? Retrieved October 1, 2025, from https://www.nsf.gov/updates-on-priorities#:~:text=Terminated%20awards-,Why%20is%20NSF%20terminating%20awards

Temple, J. (2025, June 2). The Trump administration has shut down more than 100 climate studies. MIT Technology Review.

Waldman, A., & Lerner, S. (2025, March 24). NIH ends future funding to study the health effects of climate change. ProPublica. https://www.propublica.org/article/nih-funding-climate-change-public-health

Stokstad, E. (2025, April 21). EPA orders staff to begin canceling research grants. Science. https://www.science.org/content/article/epa-orders-staff-begin-canceling-research-grants

Mello-Klein, C. (2025, June 10). The proposed NASA budget cuts would decimate American science, an expert says. Northeastern University News. https://news.northeastern.edu/2025/06/10/proposed-nasa-budget-cuts-impact/#:~:text=President%20Donald%20Trump%20has%20proposed,$24.9%20billion%20to%20$18.8%20billion

NASA. (2025, May 30). About NASA's Earth Science Division. NASA Science. https://science.nasa.gov/earth-science/programs/

www.ingramcontent.com/pod-product-compliance
Lightning Source LLC
LaVergne TN
LVHW052306200926
848481LV00002B/479
9798994970546